Forensic Investigation of Sex Crimes and Sexual Offenders

Forensic Investigation of Sex Crimes and Sexual Offenders

Chris Rush Burkey
Tusty ten Bensel
Jeffery T. Walker

Series Editor:
Larry S. Miller

Routledge
Taylor & Francis Group

LONDON AND NEW YORK

First published 2014 by Anderson Publishing

Published 2015 by Routledge
2 Park Square, Milton Park, Abingdon, Oxon OX14 4RN

and by Routledge
711 Third Avenue, New York, NY 10017, USA

Routlege is an imprint of the Taylor & Francis Group, an infoma business

British Library Cataloguing-in-Publication Data
A catalogue record for this book is available from the British Library

Library of Congress Cataloging-in-Publication Data
A catalog record for this book is available from the Library of Congress

ISBN 978-0-323-22804-6 (pbk)

CONTENTS

CHAPTER *1*

Sex Crimes and Offenders

On January 4, 1974, an eighteen-year-old freshman studying at the University of Washington was assaulted in her basement apartment. The perpetrator entered her bedroom through a window, struck the sleeping victim in the head with a metal rod from the bed frame, and sexually assaulted her with a foreign object. As a result, the victim suffered extensive internal injuries, permanent brain damage, and remained unconscious for approximately ten days. About a month later, the perpetrator broke into another victim's home, beat her unconscious, removed her night gown and hung it in the closet, dressed her in another outfit, made her bed, and wrapped the victim in sheets before carrying her out of the house. The victim's skull and mandibles were recovered months later, along with partial remains of three other victims, who also exhibited extensive physical injuries from a blunt object. These assaults were a few of the first documented string of victims for serial killer, rapist, and kidnapper, Theodore Robert Cowell—also known as Ted Bundy.

Figure 1.1 Ted Bundy mug shot.

Bundy was characterized as a handsome, charming, confident man who used his friendly demeanor to gain the trust of his young victims. His female victims had striking similarities—they were typically white, slim, single females with long hair, parted in the middle. At times, Bundy would approach his victims in public places, faking an injury, and take them to more secluded locations. Other times, like the cases discussed above, Bundy would break into homes/apartments and bludgeon the victims to death while they were sleeping. There is no official consensus on when Bundy began kidnapping, raping, and killing his victims or how many fell prey to his crimes over the years. He told varying accounts of his criminal career when authorities pressed for information.

Figure 1.2 Ted Bundy as he appeared in court.

The attacks committed by this perpetrator culminated in a frenzied spree that began in the early morning hours of January 15, 1978. One of Bundy's final and notorious crimes was the murder and rape of four female students at Florida State University in Tallahassee. He gained access to their sorority house by jimmying a faulty door lock located at the back entry of the sorority house. Once inside, Bundy maliciously bludgeoned his victims one-by-one as they slept: two were strangled to death, one was also sexually assaulted; the other two received serious head and facial injuries but managed to survive. The attacks occurred within a fifteen-minute time frame and within earshot of dozens of witnesses who were unable to hear the attacks. After leaving the sorority house, the perpetrator traveled eight blocks and assaulted another woman. This victim was also bludgeoned and sustained multiple skull and facial fractures, yet she too survived the attack. On February 9, 1978, a twelve-year-old middle school student was summoned to the school office to retrieve a missing purse. Her remains were found seven weeks later in a pig shed thirty miles from her home in Lake City, Florida. She was to be the final victim of a serial rapist and murderer who, upon his arrest on February 15, 1978, was responsible for the murders of at least thirty-five women and girls, although circumstantially linked to as many as 115 victims. In 1978, Bundy was executed for the murder of several victims across as many as seven states in four years.

Only a few years earlier, another predator had begun collecting victims in Waterloo, Iowa. Unlike Bundy, this predator targeted adolescents and young adult males. He used his position as a restaurant manager to entice young male employees into his basement "club," allowing them to drink alcohol before making sexual advances toward them. Two of the victims reported their attacker, who was eventually sentenced to ten years in an Iowa state penitentiary for the crime of sodomy. After serving only eighteen months of his ten-year sentence, he was released on parole and immediately returned to his hometown of Chicago, Illinois. Over the next few years, other adolescent victims reported sexual assaults by the perpetrator, but the charges in each case were dropped for various reasons. Then, on January 2, 1972, a fifteen-year-old youth was picked up at a Greyhound bus terminal and lured to the predator's home with the offer of a place to sleep until his connecting bus departed the following morning; however, by then the young man was dead.

This was the first confirmed murder committed by the perpetrator who would eventually rape and kill thirty-three more young men between the ages of fourteen and twenty-one. On December 20, 1978, the arrogant offender invited two police officers into his home. Upon entering the residence, the officers recognized what they believed to be the smell of decaying flesh. The following day, a search warrant was executed, and human bones were found on the premises. Eventually, twenty-nine victims were found buried on the property of the home owned by the predator, twenty-six of whom were buried in the crawl space beneath the house. The remains of one victim were found beneath the floorboards, between the joists of the dining room; another was buried beneath a barbeque grill in the back garden, and a third was located beneath the concrete floor of the garage. During his confession on December 22, 1978, the perpetrator admitted to having thrown the bodies of his last five victims off of a bridge into the Des Plaines River after having run out of room to bury any more bodies in the crawlspace. Investigation revealed some of the bodies had ligatures still tied in place around the necks, while others had gags in the mouth or throat in a manner similar to that described by previous victims who survived his attacks. It was determined that the cause of death for most of the victims was manual strangulation or asphyxiation that occurred while the victims were being raped—a technique the perpetrator referred to as his "rope trick."

A decade later, in Milwaukee, Wisconsin, another predator surfaced. Although he had committed his first murder in 1978 at the age of eighteen, the true nature of the sexual motivation behind his crimes began to manifest in 1986 when he was arrested for indecent exposure after masturbating in front of two boys. Two years later, in September of 1988, he was arrested for the crime of drugging and sexually assaulting a thirteen-year-old boy. Shortly after being released from a work release camp, he began a string of sexual assaults and murders that continued until his arrest in July of 1991.

On May 27, 1991, a fourteen-year-old boy (coincidentally, the younger brother of the September, 1988 victim) was found naked, heavily drugged, and bleeding from the rectum, wandering the streets of the predator's neighborhood. The women who found the youngster called police, who arrived to find the perpetrator present at the scene with the young man he had assaulted. He explained to police the youth was his nineteen-year-old boyfriend and they were involved in a drunken domestic dispute. The police did not verify the identity of the youth, nor did they run a background check that would have revealed that the youth was being released into the care of a convicted sex offender on parole. After returning with the boy to his apartment, the perpetrator raped, killed, and dismembered the victim.

Between May and July of 1991, the predator began a quest for the ultimate "sex slave." He began trolling for victims in gay bars within the community and luring willing partners back to his apartment with the invitation of sex, drugs, and alcohol. After having sex with his victims, he would drug them to the point of unconsciousness. He would then drill holes in the victims' skulls and inject the frontal lobes with acid or boiling water in an effort to create a wholly complicit, controllable sexual partner. During this period, the perpetrator was killing an average of one victim per week using this method. The string of assaults and murders came to an end on July 22, 1991, but not until he had claimed the lives of seventeen known victims.

Society often leaps to the conclusion that all sex crimes involve similar levels of atrocity. The aforementioned cases briefly discussed the acts of Theodore "Ted" Bundy, John Wayne Gacy, and Jeffrey Dahmer—names that have become synonymous with serial sex crimes. This presumption, however, overlooks the fact that most sex crimes do not involve murder, rarely involve the victimization of a stranger, go undetected by authorities, and are hardly ever sensationalized.

Figure 1.3 John Wayne Gacy in clown costume.

1.1 INTRODUCTION

Sex crimes are among the most publicized crimes in our society. High profile cases such as Ted Bundy, John Wayne Gacy, and Jeffrey Dahmer reinforce the public's fear of sex offenders. When these crimes are exposed in the media, it shocks our moral consciousness and we immediately become concerned about the safety of our families, friends, and loved ones. This book focuses on understanding the nature of sex crimes and those who commit these crimes. Many questions arise when we think about sex offenders. Are sex offenders really as dangerous as the media portrays? How prevalent are these types of offenders? Do they run rampant throughout our communities? Do they hide in alleyways and behind bushes awaiting their next target? In this chapter, we answer some these questions by addressing the nature of sex crimes, statistics related to these offenses, theories of sex crimes, and how these crimes are discovered. We conclude the chapter by discussing the various types of sex offenses and their definitions.

Figure 1.4 Gacy mug shot.

Figure 1.5 Jeffrey Dahmer yearbook photo.

Figure 1.6 Jeffrey Dahmer mug shot.

1.2 WHAT IS SEXUAL ASSAULT VICTIMIZATION?

Sex crimes can be broken down into several forms such as forcible rape, attempted rape, statutory rape, sexual assault, child sexual abuse, incest, and child pornography. In many states' statutes, the term *rape* has been replaced with *sexual assault*, complying with the recent trends of a gender-neutral approach. Originally under common law, rape was defined as the unlawful carnal knowledge (i.e., vaginal penetration) by force or threat of a woman by an offender who is not the victim's husband. **Rape** is now considered to be sexual intercourse and/or contact without the consent of the alleged victim, wherein the act involves violence or force, duress, or fear of harm. This definition now includes penetration against both males and females, and also includes other types of penetration such as oral, digital, and anal. The National Crime Victimization Survey (NCVS) defines rape as the:

> ...unlawful penetration of a person against the will of the victim, with use or threatened use of force, or attempting such an act. Rape includes psychological coercion and physical force, and forced sexual intercourse means vaginal, anal, or oral penetration by the offender. Rape also includes incidents where penetration is from a foreign object (e.g., a bottle), victimizations against male and female victims, and both heterosexual and homosexual rape.

States may differ in their legal definitions of rape; however, most states will share commonalities of what constitutes this behavior. First, rape occurs when there is nonconsensual contact or penetration between the penis and the mouth, vulva, or anus. This could also include nonconsensual contact or penetration with a finger, hand, or foreign object. Second, most laws will include that force or the threat of force must have occurred to be considered a rape. Third, contact and/or penetration must have occurred without the consent of the victim or when the victim was unable to give consent (i.e., under the influence of drugs or alcohol, or asleep).

Rape may come in a variety of forms such as attempted rape, sexual assault, statutory rape, and date rape. **Attempted rape** includes both the physical attempt of a sexual act and verbal threats of rape. **Sexual assault** typically occurs when someone touches any part of another person's body in a sexual manner without the person's consent. The NCVS defines sexual assault as:

> *a wide range of victimizations, separate from rape or attempted rape. These crimes include attacks or attempted attacks generally involving unwanted sexual contact between a victim and offender. Sexual assault may or may not involve force and includes grabbing or fondling. Sexual assault also includes verbal threats.*

Statutory Rape, or unlawful sexual intercourse, refers to sexual intercourse with a person below the legal age of consent, which is typically between the ages of 14 and 17. Regardless of whether or not an underage person knowingly, willingly, and with mutual consent, participated in sexual intercourse with an adult, and refuses to cooperate with the state, charges can still be filed against the adult involved. There are additional laws and penalties imposed when a person of authority such as a teacher, priest, or member of the community held in high esteem engages in sexual relations with any person under the age of 18. Another form of rape, which typically occurs among acquaintances, is **date rape.** Date rape is considered a sexual assault by an individual with whom the victim carries on a dating relationship and the assault takes place within the context of the relationship.

While all sex crimes are egregious in nature, when these crimes are committed against children, it provokes a different type of outrage among the public. **Child sexual abuse** encompasses various types of sexual activity involving a child, including acts such as voyeurism, sexual dialogue, fondling, touching of genitals, rape (vaginal, anal, and/or oral) and forcing a child to participate in prostitution or pornography. Some of the most common acts of child abuse include molestation, incest, and child pornography. Molestation is considered sexual acts with individuals under the age of 18. This includes such acts as touching and or exposure of private parts, pornographic pictures, and rape. In over half of the molestation cases reported to law enforcement officials, the offender is somehow related to the victim. Some cases are considered **incest**, a sexual relationship between two family members (i.e. parent, aunt, uncle, sister, brother). Child abuse cases of incest involve an adult relative and a child under the age of 18. In addition to molestation and incest, possession and or distribution of **child pornography** is another form of child sexual abuse. If anyone younger than 18 years of age is depicted in photographs or electronic images nude (or even partially clothed in some states), it can be considered child pornography.

With recent advancements in technology, child pornographic images can be distributed through sexting. **Sexting** is a term used to describe sexually explicit text messages or images. With the amount of underage cell phone owners rapidly increasing, it is not surprising that teen sexting is a common occurrence. While it is currently not against the law to send sexually explicit texts in the form of words, it is against the law to transmit sexually natured images of anyone under the age of 18. Teens in many states have already been arrested, convicted, or are facing child pornography charges for sending sexually natured images of themselves or others through texts.

Sex offenses come in various forms and no one is immune to victimization. Children, adults, the elderly, males, and females are all susceptible to this type of crime. Awareness of the law and types of abuse provides insight into when a sex crime has occurred so it may be reported and properly handled by authorities.

1.3 NATURE OF THE PROBLEM

Sexual victimization is a widespread problem that impacts many individuals across a lifespan. According to the National Violence Against Women Survey (NVAW), over 300,000 women and approximately 100,000 men are forcibly raped each year in the United States (Gonzales, Schefield, & Schmitt, 2006). It is estimated that one in five women (22 million) and one in 71 men (1.6 million) have experienced an attempted or completed rape at least once in their lifetime (Black et al., 2011). Further, approximately three-quarters of female victims are sexually assaulted before they are 25 years old, one-third of female victims are raped at 18 years old or younger, and one-fourth of male victims are raped when they are 10 years old or younger.

Contrary to popular belief, the majority of victims are sexually assaulted by a known offender. From 2005–2010, in the majority of sexually violent cases, the victims knew their attackers (Black, Basile, Breidling, Smith, Walters, Merrick, Chen, & Stevens, 2011). In addition, 34 percent of sexual victimizations were committed by a significant other (i.e., former or current spouse, boyfriend, or girlfriend), about six percent of victims were sexually assaulted by a relative, and 38 percent were victimized by a friend or acquaintance. Alternatively, only 22 percent of victims were sexually assaulted by a stranger. Snyder's (2000) study of National Incident Based Reporting System (NIBRS) data from 12 states reaffirms these results, suggesting that the majority of victims were attacked by an acquaintance. Given the relationship between offenders and victims, it is not surprising that 70 percent of sexual assaults reported to police occurred in the residence of the victim, the offender, or that of another individual (Snyder, 2000). These demographic and environmental data suggest that victims of rape are often attacked within a social context, in the homes of family or friends by someone they know.

1.3.1 National Data Sources on Sex Crimes

The most common forms of data collection on sexual offenses are the Uniform Crime Report (UCR) and the National Crime Victimization Survey (NCVS). The **Uniform Crime Report (UCR)** was established in 1929 by the International Association of Chiefs of Police to collect crime statistics in the United States. In 1930, the FBI took on the task of collecting, publishing, and archiving data from law enforcement agencies across the country on violent crime and property crimes. Eight index crimes are collected from the FBI, including murder, non-negligent manslaughter, forcible rape, robbery, aggravated assault, burglary, larceny-theft, motor vehicle theft, and arson.

The UCR counts one offense for each female victim of a forcible rape, attempted forcible rape, or assault with intent to rape, regardless of the victim's age. A rape by force involving a female victim and a familial offender is counted as a forcible rape and not an act of incest.

All other crimes of a sexual nature are considered to be Part II offenses; as such, the UCR Program collects only arrest data for those crimes. The offense of statutory rape, in which no force is used but the female victim is under the age of consent, is included in the arrest total for the sex offenses category. Sexual attacks on males are counted as aggravated assaults or sex offenses, depending on the circumstances and the extent of any injuries.

The UCR was established to provide reliable crime statistics; however, many weaknesses are present within the data collection process. The most common criticism associated with UCR is that it represents only reported crimes. The amount of unreported crime varies across crime types; yet, it is estimated that about half of all crimes do not appear in the UCR. Since sex offenses are the most underreported crimes to law enforcement, the UCR statistics for rape are certainly lower than what actually exists. Additionally, the UCR only accounts for the most serious crime; therefore, in an incident where multiple crimes occurred, the less severe crimes are discounted. For example, in the case of a burglary, rape, and murder, the murder would be the only crime counted in the UCR—ultimately underreporting the lesser crimes.

The **National Crime Victimization Survey (NCVS)** began in 1973 as the National Crime Survey through the U.S. Bureau of the Census. In 1992–1993, the survey was redesigned and renamed the National Crime Victimization Survey. The purpose of redesigning the NCVS was to obtain more information concerning various types of crimes. The survey collects information from a nationally representative sample of individuals aged 12 and older who live in U.S. households. NCVS collects specific information regarding the victim, the perpetrator, and the crime. This survey is known to yield more accurate statistics compared to the UCR. This is especially true with regard to crimes beyond the scope of the UCR's eight index crimes, as well as crimes generally not reported to police, such as sex offenses and domestic violence.

The NCVS may acquire more detailed and extensive information than the UCR; however, when assessing sex crimes, three main limitations to this data collection process exist. First, the NCVS excludes crimes against children under the age of 12; therefore, any sexual abuse experienced by younger children is not represented in this data.

Second, The NCVS is based on a random sample of the population and does not collect reports for all types of sex crimes. The survey is, therefore, subject to potential problems in sampling and survey biases. Additionally, the sampling size of the NCVS has been declining over the years and some observers have begun to question its representation of the U.S. population.

Although the UCR and NCVS are two of the primary data sources used in sex offending and victimization research, other sources are available, such as the National Violence Against Women Survey (NVAWS), the Sexual Experiences Survey (SES), the National College Women Sexual Victimization Study (NCWSV), and the National Study of Drug or Alcohol Facilitated, Incapacitated, and Forcible Rape. All these studies were conducted in the mid-to-late 1990s, with the exception of the NCWSV which was carried out in 2007.

The statistics discussed above give only a glimpse of the prevalence of sex crimes in the United States. Because sex crimes are the most under reported crimes to law enforcement officials we are unaware of the full extent of these crimes. We must, however, take advantage of the statistics and knowledge available to assist in providing a better understanding of these offenders and their crimes. For years, researchers have theorized various explanations as to why some people commit sex crimes. The following section focuses on the most prominent theories proposed in recent years.

1.4 THEORIES OF SEX CRIMES

Criminologists have attempted to explain the development of sexual offending behaviors for many years. Theories associated with sexual offending can be divided into two distinctive groups—Single Factor Theories and Multifactor Theories. **Single Factor Theories** attempt to explain why some individuals commit sex crimes according to one factor. These factors include biological, learning, cultural, and intimacy explanations for sex crimes. While single factor theories are somewhat limited, they provide the foundation for many of the modern multifactor theories, which are later discussed.

1.4.1 Single Factor Theories

Some researchers suggest that certain **biological** factors, such as hormones, contribute to why individuals engage in sex offending behaviors.

Perhaps most common within this category is the role of high testosterone levels, which are found to be associated with increased sex drive and aggression. Additionally, some biological theories suggest that certain individuals may be predisposed toward problematic sexual behaviors because of physiologically or biologically predetermined sexual appetites or sexual preferences. These offenses are often viewed as opportunistic crimes committed by individuals who could not control their behaviors or sexual desires. Previous research on rape offenders, focusing on the role of brain dysfunction, innate mating rituals, sex hormones, neurotransmitters, and the limbic system in promoting sex crimes has found little empirical support for uncontrollable sexual desires of offenders (Fazel et al., 2007; Lalumiere, Harris, Quinsey, & Rice, 2005; Money, 1990; Revitch, 1988). Findings from these studies suggest only limited support for the role of biology in sexual offending. This biological approach provides some understanding to causes of sex offending; however, psychologists have offered alternative explanations for criminal rape.

In a psychological spectrum, sex offenders' behavior originates with issues in childhood that affect their attachments to others, social skills development, and personality traits (Alley, 2006; Chichester, 2006; Howells, Day, & Wright, 2004; Hudson & Ward, 2000; Knight & Sims-Knight, 2004; McClintock, 1995; Ward & Sorbello, 2003). These antisocial behaviors could be products of sexual and physical abuses and neglect during childhood, which impede the development of proper attachments to others, and normative social skills. These experiences can also result in uninhibited or improper responses to opportunities and situations in which offending may occur.

Several factors have been significantly associated with childhood abuse and could result in social incompetencies such as cognitive distortions, a lack of empathy, a lack of intimacy, exaggerated emotions in terms of depression and/or anger, loneliness, and impulsivity, all of which either contribute to or facilitate antisocial behavior and sex offending. Childhood abuses and problematic attachments may lead individuals to have a variety of problems related to intimacy in adult relationships, and ultimately these **intimacy deficits** may lead individuals to engage in sexually abusive behavior. For example, insecurely attached persons may want to be emotionally close to others but avoid closeness out of a fear of being rejected or hurt. In turn, some of these individuals may attempt to establish inappropriately close relationships with children (with whom they may feel safe or less intimidated) and they may ultimately have inappropriate sexual contact with them. Those with dismissive attachment styles may have no desire to become close or intimate with others and may even harbor negative, angry, and hostile feelings toward various types of individuals. Subsequently, they may act out their anger or hostility in a sexually aggressive manner, such as in the case of violent stranger rape.

In addition, early sexual experiences, brought on by childhood abuse, may result in **conditioning** sexual fantasies and operant **learning opportunities** for future crimes. Conditioning occurs when an individual's sexual interests or arousal patterns become strengthened through certain types of experiences wherein the behavior is positively reinforced. For example when someone masturbates to fantasies that are deviant, this act tends to strengthen interests or arousal in the unhealthy or inappropriate fantasies, which has the potential to lead to offending. These circumstances tend to provide techniques and rationalizations that promote sex offending and the "cycle of violence" (Beech & Ward, 2004; Howells, Day, & Wright, 2004; Siegert & Ward, 2003). For example, a father who commits domestic violence in the home is modeling hostile and aggressive attitudes and behaviors toward women. Youth who are exposed to this kind of environment may learn to act in a similar manner as part of their developmental experiences.

Another way in which theorists have attempted to explain the causes of sex offending emphasizes the role of **societal factors** and cultural influences, norms, and messages. For example, some theorists suggest that the ways in which women and children are portrayed as submissive and passive through advertisements, television programs, and movies may contribute to sexual violence. Feminist scholars claim sexual violence against women is a way to express dominance over another, especially in patriarchal societies (Brownmiller, 1975; Copelon, 1994; MacKinnon, 1989). Historically, men have created laws to mimic their own ideals, values, and interpretation of how the government should be regulated. Feminist patriarchal jurisprudence maintains that laws are created by men for men to exercise their power over weaker groups (i.e., women and minorities) (Brownmiller, 1975; MacKinnon, 1989). Thus, violence against women, both sexually and domestically, is a broader manifestation of social systems built by men. This line of research argues rape serves as a social control mechanism for men to instill fear and terror in women, which allows men to retain their social dominance in society and assert their power over women—hegemonic masculinity (Brownmiller, 1975; MacKinnon, 1989; Tosh, 2004).

This perspective also argues the need for men to control and dominate women is typically a learned behavior developed through social interactions. Gender role distinctions play a crucial part in how individuals view their role in society. These roles are not innate but developed through societal definitions. Throughout childhood and adult experiences, men learn to "act like men"—strong, intellectual, tough, dominant, callous, and persuasive, while women learn to "be women"—nurturing, kind, sensitive, submissive, and weak. Men develop a sense of entitlement over others through various group activities, such as athletics, fraternities, and men's clubs, where they fear humiliating themselves in front of other men (Kimmel, 2005). They are consistently competing against each other and fear being seen as "wimps" or "sissies" in front of their friends or colleagues, especially in front of those who share a common bond (i.e., athletics, fraternities). It creates an environment where men are expected to be tough, dominant, and aggressive toward others, especially women who are typically weaker and easily restrained by men.

These are just a few examples of some of the single factor or more narrowly focused theories proposed over the years in an attempt to explain why people commit sex offenses. Many aspects of those theories continue to be influential; however, none of these theories fully explain why all individuals engage in sex offending behaviors. Additionally, it is questionable whether any one single factor theory can adequately explain why someone may commit a sex crime. The causes of sex offending can be more complex. Additionally, these single factor theories have paved the way for continuing and expanded efforts in understanding this problem—they lay the foundation for multifactor theories.

1.4.2 Multifactor Theories

More recent theories have proposed an integrated, multifactorial approach to explaining the initiation and the continuation of sex crimes. Some of these multifactor theories include Integrated, Relapse Prevention, Self-Regulation Model, and Pathways Model.

According to the **Integrated Theory**, sexual offending behaviors are the result of a combination of biological, developmental, environmental/cultural influences, individual vulnerabilities, and situational factors. It suggests that negative developmental influences that occur early in life, such as maltreatment or exposure to violence in the home, have a significant impact on one's ability to form close and meaningful relationships. Additionally, these influences negatively affect internal characteristics related to sexually deviant behavior such as problem solving, emotional management, self-esteem, self-control, and coping skills.

Additional difficulties with adjustment during adolescence, such as peer rejection and social isolation only exacerbate existing problems and vulnerabilities. This makes it increasingly difficult for these individuals to effectively deal with the physical and hormonal changes, which emerge during puberty. If individuals are already vulnerable, they do not properly learn healthy methods of meeting their sexual, social, and psychological needs. This is particularly true when significant stressors and difficult situations arise in their lives. They are likely to resort to unhealthy means of meeting their needs and managing their emotions and behaviors. For example, to deal with unpleasant feelings like anger, rejection, or loneliness, they may masturbate to deviant fantasies, which reinforce the deviant fantasies even more. A compounding variable of exposure to certain cultural messages, such as those that condone aggression and objectification of women, only increases the likelihood of sex offending behaviors. Through a complex interaction of these and other factors, both internal and external, individuals may ultimately act out in a sexually aggressive manner.

Another multifactor theory suggests that a combination of three primary clusters of risk factors (motivators, disinhibitors, and opportunities) increases the likelihood that an individual will become sexually aggressive toward others. More specifically, the interaction of these risk factors results in two pathways to sex offending: the sexually promiscuous pathway and the hostile masculinity pathway.

Similar to the Integrated Theory, the **Confluence Model** is based in part on the premise that adverse developmental experiences such as physical or sexual abuse during childhood have a detrimental impact on the ways in which individuals view themselves (and others) and their ability to form meaningful and healthy relationships. Theorists further propose that an antisocial or delinquent orientation often results from these experiences. Depending upon other situational or environmental variables and influences, the individual either develops into a person who uses sexual conquest and sometimes coercive tactics as a means of elevating his or her peer status and self-esteem, or someone who holds strong adversarial and mistrustful attitudes about women (or men) and uses sexual aggression as a means to dominate, control, and humiliate.

One of the most common multifactor theories is based on the model of **Relapse Prevention**. Relapse Prevention is the primary theoretical framework upon which most sex offender treatment programs have been established over the past several years. It describes not only the characteristics and factors that may predispose individuals to commit sex offenses, but also the process by which sex offending develops. According to the Relapse Prevention model, sex offending is the end result of a common chain of events that leads to offending. This chain of events begins with the person experiencing some type of negative emotion. This is followed by deviant fantasies and the use of cognitive distortions to justify or rationalize these fantasies. In turn, the fantasies lead to premeditated planning about a particular offense. Finally, after disinhibiting one's self in some manner, the individual commits a sex offense.

The premise underlying the Relapse Prevention model suggests that a number of identifiable precursors, both early and more immediate, are commonly associated with offending behaviors for most individuals. Included among the earlier precursors are family dysfunction and chaos, childhood maltreatment such as neglect or physical and sexual abuse, sexual anxiety, and marital conflict. Anger problems, assertiveness and social skills deficits, impaired empathy, emotional management difficulties, personality disorders, and substance abuse are among the more immediate factors preceding an offense.

Based on this theoretical framework, interventions are designed to teach offenders to identify and address the risk factors that are believed to be linked to their offending, and to help them learn how to interrupt that predictable chain of events that leads to offending. Although this theoretical model has remained very popular in the sex offender management field for quite some time, some experts in recent years have challenged it, largely because it assumes that the sequence of emotions, fantasies, thoughts, and behaviors is equally applicable to all individuals.

The **Self-Regulation Model** considers individuals' different motivations and self-management skills. This model addresses the role of agency- and self-regulation in the offense process. Self-Regulation suggests that offenders are seeking to achieve specific goals and due to the desire to achieve these goals, offenders respond to the meaning of events in relation to their own knowledge, values, and societal interactions. In other words, this model takes into account the strong contextual element involved in the process of sex offending and/or desisting. The models' developers use four categories to explain and characterize the sex offending process for different individuals:

- Avoidant—Passive: Characterized by the desire to avoid sex offending; however, the individual lacks the coping skills to prevent the behavior from taking place (under-regulation).
- Avoidant—Active: The direct attempt to control deviant thoughts and fantasies through the use of ineffective or counterproductive strategies (misregulation).
- Approach—Automatic: The desire to sexually offend along with impulsive and poorly planned behavior (under-regulation).
- Approach—Explicit: The desire to sexually offend, the use of careful planning to carry out the offense, and the presence of harmful goals regarding sexual offending.

One of the more current theories, **Pathways Model**, recognizes that not all individuals follow the same "path" to offending. These multiple pathways are influenced by complex interactions of interpersonal emotional, biological, physiological, cultural, and environmental variables. The Pathways Model suggests that individuals experience difficulties in four clusters of psychological problems. These problems include cognitive distortions, emotional management difficulties, intimacy and social skills deficits, and deviant or unhealthy sexual scripts. These psychological issues explain the primary reasons that individuals engage in sex offending behaviors. So depending upon what their main deficits are, they fall into one of the following five pathways:

- Multiple dysfunctional mechanisms pathway
- Deviant sexual scripts pathway
- Intimacy deficits pathway
- Emotional dysregulation pathway
- Antisocial cognitions pathway

This conceptualization offers a range of relatively distinct but also interacting explanations for why those who sexually offend do what they do. Similar to and building upon other multifactor theories, the Pathways Model takes into account a number of characteristics or risk factors that appear to be common among sex offenders. What seems to set it apart from some of the other theories is that it fully considers the diverse nature of offenders, rather than assuming that all offenders follow the same or very similar paths to offending.

There is no simple answer as to why people commit sex crimes. Researchers and other experts in the field have dedicated their life's work attempting to find the answer. The most plausible explanation involves interactions among numerous variables across a variety of domains—revealing that there is no single pathway that can be established to explain this behavior for all sex offenders.

1.5 HOW SEX CRIMES ARE TYPICALLY DISCOVERED

Unlike the case studies discussed at the beginning of the chapter, most sex crimes are not discovered during the investigation of a murder. Yes, this does occur during some homicide investigations; however, the majority of sex crimes are discovered when a victim chooses to reveal his or her abuse to law enforcement officials. Once a victim is brave enough to tell the story, law enforcement can take the proper steps in establishing whether or not a sex crime occurred. In some cases, the investigation of one sex crime leads to the discovery of other sex crimes and victims. Unfortunately, many individuals refuse to report abuse for reasons discussed earlier in this chapter. This is the main reason why sex crimes are among the most difficult crimes for law enforcement to discover. If individuals do not come forward to reveal their abuse, these crimes go undetected. Researchers are attempting to address the various reasons why individuals fear reporting their abuse and propose measures by which to relieve the fear associated with reporting a sex crime. Some researchers speculate that specific training in counseling and interview techniques within the law enforcement community may assist in providing a suitable environment for victims to feel safe when exposing their sexual abuse. In addition to specific law enforcement training, the public must be aware of the various acts that constitute a sex crime so they may be better recognized and reported.

REFERENCES

Greenfield, (1997).

Department of Justice. (2005) <http://www.justice.gov>.

UCR. <http://www.fib.gov>.

NOVA. <http://www.trynova.org>.

NOVA

Rain (2011).

Ward,, T., & Gannon, T. (2006). Rehabilitation, etiology, and self regulation: The comprehensive good lives model of treatment for sexual offenders. *Aggression and Violent Behavior, 11*, 77−94.

Gonzales, Schefield & Schmitt, 2006.

Black, Basile, Breidling, Smith, Walters, Merrick, et al., 2011 National Intimate Partner and Sexual Violence Survey.

Snyder's (2000).

National Crime Victimization Survey (2005) < http://www.icpsr.umich.edu/icpsrweb/NACJD/studies?q = %22national + crime + victimization + survey%22 >.

Fazel, et al. (2007).

Lalumiere, M., Harris, G., Quinsey, V., & Rice, M. (2005). *The causes of rape: Understanding individual differences in male propensity for sexual aggression.* Washington, DC: American Psychological Association.

Money (1990).

Revitch, E., & Schlesinger, L. B. (1988). Clinical reflections on sexual aggression. *Annals of the New York Academy of Sciences.*

Alley (2006).

Chichester (2006).

Howells, Day, & Wright (2004). *Affect Emotions and Sex Offending* (Vol. 10, Number 2, June 2004, pp. 179−195(17)). Taylor Francis Group.

Ward, T., & Hudson, S. M. (2000). A self-regulation model of relapse prevention. *Remaking relapse prevention with sex offenders: A sourcebook, 79*−101.

Knight, R. A., & Sims-Knight, J. E. (2005). Testing an etiological model for male juvenile sexual offending against females. *Journal of Child Sexual Abuse, 13*(3−4), 33−55.

McClintock (1995).

Ward, T., & Sorbello, L. (2003). Explaining child sexual abuse: Integration and elaboration. In T. Ward, D. R. Laws, & S. M. Hudson (Eds.), *Sexual deviance: Issues and controversies in sexual deviance* (pp. 3−20). London: Sage.

Beech, A. R., & Ward, T. (2004). The integration of etiology and risk in sex offenders: A theoretical model. *Aggression and Violent Behavior, 10*, 31−63.

Siegert, R. J., & Ward, T. (2003). Back to the future: evolutionary explanations of rape. In T. Ward, D. R. Laws, & S. M. Hudson (Eds.), *Sexual deviance: Issues and controversies* (pp. 45−64). Thousand Oaks, CA7: Sage.

Brownmiller, S. (1975). Against our will: men, women, and rape. *Ballentine Books.*

Copelon, R. (1994). Surfacing gender: reconceptualizing crimes against women in time of war. In A. Stiglmayer, M. Faber, & R. Gutman (Eds.), (pp. 197−218). University of Nebraska Press.

MacKinnon (1989).

CHAPTER 2

Typology of Sexual Offenders

2.1 CASE STUDY 1

Male: "So what time are you planning on heading over?"
Female: "Are you sure? Like, I just feel... I mean, I don't want you lying to your mom. I mean, it's like..."
Male: "No, it's all right. She's gone in a sales meeting, like all day."
Female: "You're sure?"
Male: "Yeah."
Female: "All right. Promise?"
Male: "Yeah."
Female: "Pinky promise!"
Male: "Yes."
Female: "Say pinky promise."
Male: "Pinky promise."
Female: "All right. Well, tell me a time."

This is an excerpt from a telephone conversation recorded by the police between 23-year-old teacher, Debra Jean Beasley Lafave and a 14-year-old student at Greco Middle School, located in Tampa, Florida.

They were in a sexual relationship in which they had sex on five occasions the week before her arrest on June 21, 2004. According to the victims' statement, he met Lafave at a football game a few months prior to their sexual encounters and later became better acquainted on a field trip, which was chaperoned by Lafave and her husband. The two exchanged phone numbers, talked frequently, and began a sexual relationship at the end of the school year. It began when Lafave invited the victim to her classroom and told him she had developed romantic feelings for him, at which time the victim reciprocated the sentiments, and the two had their first kiss. Approximately one week later, she drove to Ocala, Florida, one hundred miles north of Tampa, where the victim was staying with his fifteen-year-old cousin. Lafave then drove the boys back to her apartment in Tampa for pizza and a movie. While the victim's cousin watched a Pay-per-View movie in the living room, Lafave took the victim to her bedroom and performed oral sex on him. The two returned downstairs, watched the rest of the movie, and then LaFave drove the boys back to Ocala, during which time, she again performed oral sex on the victim in the back seat.

On June 14, 2004, the victim was helping Lafave clean her classroom for the summer and the two engaged in sexual intercourse for the first time. The following day, Lafave drove the victim to Ocala to visit his cousin. Upon arriving, she gave the keys to the Rodeo to the fifteen-year-old cousin and climbed into the back seat with the victim. The two engaged in sexual intercourse in the back seat of the vehicle as the cousin drove the trio around the town. This was the first of three such sexual encounters between Lafave and the victim during that week.

Figure 2.1 Debra Lafave.

It was only after the cousin's mother witnessed the three together, in Ocala, that the details of the encounters became known to others. The cousin's mother contacted the victim's mother, who immediately confronted her son about his being in the company of the teacher. The youth bragged about his relationship with the "hot teacher," and police were immediately contacted by the victim's parent. Once the authorities were involved, they convinced the victim to record a series of phone calls with Lafave, with the goal of gathering evidence regarding their sexual relationship. It began with surveillance videos that showed the teacher—wearing a short, halter-top sun dress—roaming through an electronics store with the boys, drinking smoothies. The video evidence, accompanied by the recorded phone conversations, exposed the sexual nature of the relationship between the student and teacher (including the opening transcript excerpt), provided enough evidence to charge Lafave with lewd and lascivious battery, and arrest her for having inappropriate sexual behaviors with a minor.

In subsequent public interviews, Lafave admitted having a sexual relationship with the victim; however, she did not accept culpability for the acts, instead blaming her behavior on a depressed mental state. When interviewed on NBC, Lafave recalled details of her own shaky past which she believes played a role in her current mental condition. While in the 8th grade, she was raped by her older boyfriend in a school bathroom. The rape was allegedly interrupted by a teacher, who dismissed the encounter and sent the students back to class. In addition, Lafave's pregnant sister was killed by a drunk driver in 2001. Lafave claimed the trauma of these events caused her to enter a state of depression—a condition later diagnosed as bipolar disorder. She suffered from hyper sexuality and was unable to rationalize the severity or the possible consequences of her actions. In 2005, Lafave pleaded guilty of Lewd or Lascivious Battery and bargained for no prison time, three years of house arrest, and seven years of probation. Her lawyer argued she was too attractive to be sentenced to prison and it would be "like putting a piece of raw meat in with the lions." FoxNews.com December 2004, Orlando Salenas - transcript.

2.2 CASE STUDY 2

On August 11, 2012, members of the Steubenville, West Virginia football team threw a party to celebrate their victory in a pre-season scrimmage game. In attendance were 17-year-old Trent Mays and

16-year-old Ma'lik Richmond, along with teammates and high school classmates. At the party there was also a 16-year-old female who, witnesses claim, was drinking large quantities of alcohol, staggering and slurring her speech, and, to the frustration of her friends, rolling on the floor. Irritated by her behavior, the victim's friends encouraged her to leave the party with them. She refused to leave and was persuaded by Mays and Richmond to go to another party. There were several photographs that later surfaced of the two males carrying the unconscious victim to their car as they left the party. While Richmond drove, Mays penetrated the victim's vagina with his fingers in the back seat.

At the second party, Mays and Richmond took the victim to the basement, got her undressed and again assaulted by digital penetration, this time by both Mays and Richmond. The two then used Mays' cellular phone to take photographs of the nude victim. Later a video also surfaced in which Mays was bragging to his friends about his encounter with the victim. When asked by one of the male party attendees whether the victim was unconscious, he answered, "She's dead as a doornail." The video was uncovered by an internet watchdog group who, calling for an investigation, posted the video on the internet.

The victim woke up the following morning naked and unable to recall the events of the previous night. She also discovered her phone, earrings, shoes, and underwear were missing. Her only recollection of the previous night was drinking alcohol, leaving a party holding hands with Mays, and later vomiting. The victim called one of her friends to pick her up and, according to the friend's statements, the victim was "a mess," wearing a vomit stained shirt inside-out. It was only after viewing pictures taken the night of the party, reading text messages that were being circulated among her peer group, and watching a video of her attack, that the victim realized she had been assaulted.

In the ensuing investigation, 17 cell phones were confiscated by law enforcement from individuals who had sent and received text messages from the perpetrators during the hours of the attack and the days that followed. A computer forensics expert, with the West Virginia Bureau of Investigation, examined the devices and more than three thousand messages were introduced as evidence at the trial. The following are excerpts from the messages that were admitted. The names of the perpetrators were a matter of public record and were used extensively by the media, in public police reports, and during the trial; however, to protect the anonymity of the victim and those juveniles involved in text messaging, names have been omitted.

2.2.1 August 12, 2012

[Contact 1] to Trent Mays:	"I'm comin with where u at?"
Mays:	"[omitted name], we're hittin it for real"
[Contact 1]:	"Wait for me lol"
[Contact 2] to Mays:	"I wanna see the vid of you hittin her with your wiener."
Mays:	"I don't know who took it lol"
[Contact 3] to Mays:	"Did you fuck her?"
Mays:	"Yes."
[Contact 3]:	"Yeah boy!"
[Contact 4] to Mays:	"Was that on the couch downstairs lmao"
Mays:	"Yes"
[Contact 4]:	"She looks dead lmao"
Mays:	"She is"
[Contact 4]:	"Shoulda moved her around and got a better angle"

Multimedia picture message was sent from Trent Mays to two contacts; picture is of the naked victim; caption reads: "Bitches is bitches. Fuck 'em"

2.2.2 August 13, 2012

[Contact 1] to Mays:	"Dude, your jizz was on her chest lol. Tell me what happened."
Mays:	"I talked her into a handy cause if she moved she'd get sick"
[Contact 5] to Mays:	"Do anything with [victim]?"
Mays:	"She was a deady, and I needed sexual attention just like u lol. I shoulda f*cked her"
Mays:	"Yeah dude it was bad, but she was naked so it was all good"
Mays:	"I fingered her before you asked though"
Mays to [Contact 6]:	"Delete that off You Tube. Coach Sac knows about it. Seriously delete it"
[Contact 6] to Mays:	"Deny to the grave"
Mays:	"Her dad knows, and if our names get brought up, if asked, she was just really drunk."
Mays:	"They know she stayed at [omitted name]'s. You just gotta say she was asleep by the time you got there."

2.2.3 August 14, 2012

[Contact 7] to Mays:	"Did anyone f*ck her?"
Mays:	"Me fingered her. That's about it."
[Contact 8] to Mays:	"What about you f***ing her in the a**?"
Mays:	"?"
[Contact 8]:	"That's what the picture is of"
Mays:	"The only pic I have is her laying on the couch"
[Contact 8]:	"Everyone was looking at the pics at [omitted name]'s"
Mays:	"Neither of those happened. I wanna see those."
[Contact 8]:	"Don't lie. I was at [omitted name]'s house."
Mays:	"If you saw them, you lied."
[Contact 8]:	"Don't lie to me. I saw the pics at [omitted name]'s. They were showing them all around."

On March 17, 2013, Trent Mays and Ma'lik Richmond were found delinquent on rape charges by a juvenile court judge (equivalent of a guilty verdict in adult criminal court). Mays was sentenced to a minimum of two years in juvenile detention, while Richmond was sentenced to a minimum of one year in juvenile detention. The exact length of their stay in a juvenile detention facility will depend on the juvenile system and the offenders' behavior while under supervision. Mays was also convicted of the use of a minor in nudity-oriented material and received an additional sentence to be served upon completion of his sentence for the rape charge. Pittsburgh Post Gazette, Torsten Ove 2013.

2.3 CASE STUDY 3

Reverend Jack Schaap, former pastor of First Baptist Church of Hammond, Indiana, pled guilty to transporting a minor across state lines with intent to engage in illegal sexual activity. Schaap was the pastor of the mega-church, one of the largest in the country, and had published books on dating and marriage during his tenure as the church leader. Schaap was also the superintendent of Chicago's Baptist school system. He began grooming his victim after she was referred to him for counseling by a concerned teacher within the school system. Meetings between the pastor and the victim began one week prior to her 17th birthday.

Figure 2.2 Jack Schaap mug shot.

During the course of his sessions with the victim, Schaap told staff members she was in need of specialized counseling and requested she be transported to private retreat centers for in-depth attention to her spiritual needs. The "retreat centers" were, in fact, private properties owned by Schaap, located out of state: a cabin in Michigan, and a vacation home in Crete, Illinois. The staff members agreed to drive the girl across state lines, where the pastor would engage in acts symbolizing a three-day period surrounding the death, burial, and resurrection of Christ; however, during this thirty-six hour period at his private cabin, he had multiple sexual encounters with the victim. In an effort to explain the need to take the girl alone to his Michigan cabin, he told his assistant her counseling would require extended periods alone to "save" her—both spiritually and literally. Investigation into Schaap's activities would later reveal pictures of the two inside his cabin in intimate poses and "French" kissing, while he touched her in a sexual manner. Schaap also expressed the need to go to his wilderness sanctuary to "spend time with God walking and praying." He continued to have frequent liaisons with the victim, including one sexual encounter that took place in his church office during a youth conference. When confronted with questions from staff members, he dismissed them by telling the parishioners she was "on her period and needed to lie down." In the process of covering up his indiscretions, Schaap even met with the victim's father to tell him that she was "doing great." Chicago Sun Times November 2013.

Figure 2.3 Reverend Jack Schaap.

Schaap and his victim also exchanged frequent letters and text messages—662 texts one month. One message from Schaap to the victim read, "Yesterday was 'off the charts!' :)))." Another message told the victim, "In our 'fantasy talk,' you have affectionately spoken of being 'my wife.' That is exactly what Christ desires for us. He wants to marry us + become eternal lovers!" Schaap's undoing began when he asked a staff member if he could erase information from his cellular phone, which was property of the church. The staff member became concerned and examined the pastor's phone and found pictures that included Schaap kissing the victim in his office. The staff member immediately contacted the police, who launched a detailed investigation. Upon realizing that Schaap met with the victim across state lines, federal agencies assumed jurisdiction over the investigation.

In 2012, Jack Schaap was fired from his position as pastor. In September of the same year, he pleaded guilty to the charge of transporting a minor across state lines with intent to engage in illegal sexual activity. Thereafter, on March 20, 2013, Schaap was sentenced to twelve years in prison and five years of supervised probation.

2.4 INTRODUCTION

There are a variety of misconceptions about sex offenders, which are typically derived from popular stereotypes. When trying to understand the typologies and motivations of sex offenders, they will rarely fit into what is portrayed in "movies." They come from varying backgrounds, socioeconomic classes, races, and genders. Their crimes have differing motives, victims, and methods. Understanding these offenders is paramount in the process of identification and prevention of sex crimes. This chapter provides a general depiction of what we know about sex offender characteristics and their crimes, which include their social, psychological, and contextual backgrounds.

2.5 TYPOLOGIES

A **typology** is the systematic classification based on common characteristics or traits. This also involves the use of such classifications to analyze and study a particular culture, groups of people, languages, and even symbols. Although sex offenders are not considered a homogenous group, researchers have attempted to classify them according to specific characteristics and behaviors. The following sections discuss the various typologies of rapists, individuals who sexually abuse children, juvenile sex offenders, female sex offenders and cyber sex offenders.

2.5.1 Rapists

The act of rape is always an aggressive behavior—one that is complex and multi-dimensional. Several classifications or typologies have been created throughout the last few decades (Guttmacher, 1952; Kopp, 1962; Gebhard, Gagnon, Pomeroy, & Christenson, 1965). Groth (1979) proposed a sex offender typology—a model used extensively by practitioners—that divided rapists into four categories: power reassurance rapists (compensatory), power assertive rapists (power, impulsive), anger retaliation rapists (power, control), and anger excitation rapists (sadistic) (Berger, 2000; Groth, 1979; Robertiello and Terry, 2007).

The **power reassurance rapists** desire dominance over another. Many times, this type of rapist will have no desire to hurt the victim, but to have sexual possession of the victim. The rapist uses sexuality to compensate feelings of inadequacy, poor social skills, strength, authority, and identity. Typically, this type of offender will use only the necessary amount of force required to achieve his or her purpose. The rapist may give the victim verbal warnings such as "Do what I say and you will not get hurt" (Groth, 1978). Some researchers describe this type of offender as having a "courtship disorder" (Freund, 1990), in which the offender lacks the ability to form a normal relationship with someone of the same age. Once they commit a rape, their feelings of inadequacy generally subside. These types of offenders portray less aggression than other types of rapists under both sexual and non-sexual circumstances. They are sometimes described as "gentleman rapists" because they normally use the least amount of force necessary to carry out the rape. Anger only arises when the victim resists. They may use verbal intimidation, physical force, or even a weapon during the assault; however, they are likely to run away if the victim screams or fights back. Additionally, power reassurance rapists typically spend only a short amount of time with their victims due to their lack of confidence and social skills necessary to interact with a sexual partner for any length of time. Victims of this type of offender, however, frequently report what may be considered "pillow talk" after the assault occurs, causing one to question this particular characteristic of the power reassurance rapist.

The **power assertive rapists** use aggressive yet non-lethal actions to display their masculinity. Their actions are committed to reassure themselves of their power as a man and stifle any inner insecurities/fears related to their manhood. These individuals are often impulsive, opportunistic, geographically mobile, under the influence of drugs or alcohol, and leave their victims emotionally traumatized. They typically meet or view their victims in a public location, such as a bar, and often rape them on the same day. These offenders are impulsive by nature; therefore, their attacks are unplanned and do not involve any type of weapon.

For both types of power rapists, sexual satisfaction is minimal and disappointing because the assault never lives up to the offender's fantasies. This is an excerpt from one of the interviews conducted by Groth (1979):

It never came down the way I imagined it would. In the fantasy, after the initial shock of the attack, I thought the victim would be more accepting and responsive, but, in reality, that was never the case. I did not have the good feelings I fantasized about. I felt let down. I didn't experience the same feelings in the actual assault that I had expected to feel. Everything was pleasurable in the fantasy, and there was acceptance, whereas in the reality of the situation, it wasn't pleasurable, and the girl was scared, not turned on to me.

When the offender reflects and finds that he is not reassured of his strength, power, and performance, he is likely to go out and find another victim who may be the "right one." This creates cycle of rapes which are repetitive, compulsive, and situated in a short timeframe. The victim of a power rapist is either the same age as the offender or younger. In addition, these rapists will target women who are weaker, more vulnerable, and smaller than the offender.

Another type of offender is the **anger retaliation rapist.** This type of rapists often use high levels of physical and sexual aggression due to their unhealthy rage. They attempt to "get even" with their victims by using sex as a weapon to punish them. The rapes often include degrading and humiliating acts and verbal language. Their actions may be premeditated or directed toward a specific individual who happens to spark their rage. Attacks by these types of rapists are considered interpersonal acts involving the need for power and aggression. Groth explains these perpetrators as the "sexual expression of aggression rather than the aggressive expression of sexuality" (Groth 1983, p. 165).

These offenders will often use degrading forms of abuse to sexually assault their victims, such as sodomy or fellatio, or even urinating, masturbating, or ejaculating on the victim. Anger retaliation rapists are typically not sexually aroused when assaulting their victims, rather they may have to masturbate or get the victim to engage in oral sex to achieve an erection. For example, in one of Groth's (1979) interviews with a rapist:

> I was enraged when I started out. I lost control and struck out with violence. After the assault I felt relieved. I felt I had gotten even. There was no sexual satisfaction; in fact, I felt disgusted. I felt relieved of the tension and anger for a while, but then it would start to build up again, little things, but I couldn't shake them off.

This type of offender will view sex as a "dirty" and "unclean" act of aggression and will use the assault as a venue to degrade, humiliate, and defile their victims. The majority of these offenders use the act of hurting and defiling the victim to release pent-up anger.

The **anger excitation rapist** or sadistic rapist becomes sexually excited by the fear and pain they inflict on their victims. Unlike the power assertive rapist, the anger excitation rapists plan their attacks with extreme precision. They typically choose victims who are strangers to them and show no remorse for their actions. They typically use weapons and even torture during the process of the rape. These individuals are more likely to bind, bite, beat and insert foreign objects into their victims. Since these types of offenders typically use torture during their assaults their actions may ultimately lead to murder.

Knight and Prentkey (1990) established perhaps the most comprehensive model of sex offender typology, with three distinct groups: opportunistic, pervasively angry, and vindictive. **Opportunistic rapists** commit their sexually natured crimes on impulse. Their offenses are unplanned, predatory types of acts that reveal no impulse control. Similar to gentleman rapists, they do not display signs of anger except when confronted with resistance. These rapists can be further sub-typed as high social competence or low social competence. The **pervasively angry rapists** typically use violence during the assault, even if the victim does not resist. If the victim does resist, this type of rapist may resort to injuring or killing the victim. Similar to the opportunistic rapist, the pervasively angry rapists have little impulse control. The **vindictive rapists** typically use their actions to humiliate and degrade their victims. They are not impulsive, but rather take their time in planning their attacks. They too can be divided into two further subgroups: the vindictive type with high social competence and the vindictive type with low social competence.

The majority of adult rapists are driven by power and control, especially in marital, acquaintance, and date rapes. Drug rapes can be either planned or unplanned. This is also true in rape during times of war. Rapes are committed against the enemy for the purpose of humiliating, destroying, and demoralizing the community's honor. Although rapes that involve power and control are the most common, the most dangerous rapists are those with sadistic tendencies. These types of rapes/rapists are much more likely to involve torture and possibly death.

2.5.2 Child Molesters

Similar to other types of sex offenders, child molesters vary in their typologies and motivations for offending. They may be male or female, homosexual, heterosexual, or bisexual, married or single, and come from any race or socioeconomic standing. Although this group of offenders is a heterogeneous population, researchers have found some common characteristics among those who prefer to sexually offend against children and/ or adolescents. These characteristics typically include lower level social skills, poor self-esteem, feelings of inadequacy, feelings of worthlessness and vulnerability, aversion to, or bad experience involving, adult relationships, view themselves as physically unattractive, and tend to be prone toward feelings of humiliation and loneliness.

In the 1980s, researchers began classifying child molesters into typologies based on sexual motivations of offending. The most common classification was proposed by Groth, Hobson, and Gary, and it stems from two basic premises. The first involves the degree to which the deviant sexual behavior is established in the abuser. The second involves the basis for psychological needs. With these basic premises

Groth and his colleagues established two categories of child molester. He labels them as either fixated offenders or regressed offenders.

Fixated offenders are those who are exclusively attracted to children. This attraction for children typically develops in early adolescence when the offender is also young. As the offenders get older, they continue to have an attraction to children as an adult. Most fixated offenders are diagnosed with **pedophilia**, defined by many medical professionals as a psychosexual disorder in which the fantasy or act of engaging in sexual activity with a pre-pubescent child is the preferred or exclusive means of achieving sexual excitement and or gratification (DSM IV). In addition to pedophilia, fixated offenders are typically unable to attain any degree of psychosexual maturity; therefore, their adulthood usually lacks age-appropriate sexual relationships.

On the other hand, **regressed offenders'** behavior usually emerges in adulthood and is typically preceded by external stressors. These stressors may be situational such as employment difficulties, marital conflict, or substance abuse. Stressors may also include mental and emotional states such as loneliness, isolation, depression, stress, anxiety, poor self-esteem, or low self-confidence. For regressed offenders, sexual interest in children is a temporary departure from the offenders' usual attraction to adult sexual relationships. In addition, they typically focus on children with whom they have easy access, such as their own children, step-children, or close relatives (niece or nephew).

The FBI expanded Groth's typologies to include seven subgroups of child molesters, including morally indiscriminate, sexually indiscriminate, and inadequate. Additions to the fixated typology include individuals who are seductive, fixated, and sadistic (see Table 2.1).

The risk level child molesters pose to society is dependent upon a variety of factors. Those who are the highest risk are fixated sex offenders, who most likely have committed multiple offenses. When combined with low social skills, child molesters who have high fixation levels tend to be most sexually deviant and victimize far more children than the other typologies.

2.5.3 Female Sex Offenders

Previous research on sex offenders has been predominantly focused on male sex offenders; therefore, very little is known about female sex

Table 2.1 The FBI Typologies of Child Molesters	
Type of Offender	Characteristics of Offenders
Situational Offenders	
Regressed	Offenders have poor coping skills, target easily accessible victims, abuse children as a substitute for adult relationships.
Morally	Offenders do not prefer children over adults yet tend to use children for their own sexual interests when no one else is available (indiscriminate).
Sexually	Offenders interested in sexual exploration and experimentation and abuse children out of boredom (indiscriminate).
Inadequate	Offenders are social misfits who are insecure, have low self-esteem, and see relationships with children as their only sexual outlet.
Preferential Offenders	
Seductive	Offenders "court" children and give them affection, attention, love, and gifts in order to carry on a "relationship" with a child.
Fixated	Offenders have poor psychosexual development, desire affection from children, and are compulsively attracted to children.
Sadistic	Offenders are aggressive, sexually excited by violence, target strangers as potential victims, and are extremely dangerous.
Robertiello and Terry 2007; Terry and Tallon 2004	

offenders. This is often due to stereotypes placed on women which do not comply with those of a sex offender. Despite recent publicized cases surrounding female sex offenders, many view women as incapable of committing such crimes. They are seen as nurturers, caregivers, and protectors. These stereotypes, along with the increase in female sex offenders in recent years, have prompted researchers to begin studying female sex offenders more closely. When compared to male sex offenders, female sex offenders are less likely to use force, more likely to initiate the deviant sexual behavior at a younger age, and often commit their crimes with another person. Additionally, female offenders are more likely to come forward and admit their wrongdoing, compared to their male counterparts.

Typologies concerning female sex offenders can be divided into three groups: teacher/lover, male coerced/male accompanied, and predisposed. The **teacher/lover** typology is an individual who abuses her position of power. These types of sex offenders do not see themselves as criminals, and often view their sexual encounters as acts of kindness. Teacher/lover offenders will seek a loving relationship with the victim, who is most often male. Most of these offenders have been in sexually abusive relationships with a former partner and deny any negative impact their behavior may have had on their victim(s). Although these types of offenders downplay their abusive actions, they are highly treatable and amenable to therapy.

Male coerced / male accompanied offenders are considered more traditional, subordinate women who are highly influenced by males they fear. They typically have lower IQs, low self-esteem, and feelings of inadequacy and powerlessness. These women often experience domestic violence within their relationships and are pushed to abuse others with their abuser. The male-coerced offenders carry out their crimes for fear of repercussion, whereas the male-accompanied offenders may be more self-motivated and enjoy the offense. Treatments for these offenders are typically centered on cognitive behavioral changes, focusing on independence from male counterparts.

Predisposed offender abuse their own children or children in their care. These offenders commit their crimes in the absence of a male accomplice. Most of the predisposed offenders were sexually abused as children, and many have psychological disorders; therefore, they find it difficult to establish healthy sexual relationships. They typically prey on children younger than six and are more likely to inflict pain upon their victims due to their propensity toward sadistic fantasies and suicidal thoughts. These offenders are difficult to treat due to their mental instability.

Along with these typologies, an angry/impulsive typology was later added by researchers. This type of female offender acts alone in an angry and impulsive manner, primarily against adult males. While this typology is rare, researchers have suggested the angry and impulsive offenders, along with the predisposed offenders, are among the most dangerous. Proposed treatment for this type of offender entails addressing past personal abuse issues, as well as implementing anger management techniques.

2.5.4 Juvenile Sex Offenders

Juveniles are not immune to committing sex offenses. Similar to adult offenders, juveniles who commit sex crimes vary in age, race, maturity, religion, and socioeconomic background. According to the UCR, juveniles are responsible for over 15% of forcible rapes and over 17% of other sexual offenses. One study on juvenile offenders found that 90 percent of juvenile sex offenders are male, and 60 percent penetrated their victims during the assault. Juvenile sex offenders usually have a history of delinquent behavior and many have difficulties with impulse control, learning disabilities, mental illnesses, and deviant sexual arousal tendencies.

Juvenile sex offender typologies are two-fold: those who abuse children and those who abuse peers/adults. Those who abuse children do not discriminate between genders and often abuse their siblings or other close relatives. They rely primarily on opportunity, bribery, trickery, and threats to sway or coerce their victims into performing sexual acts. These individuals often exhibit low social skills and self-esteem and battle various levels of depression. On the other hand, juveniles who target peers and/or adults do so during the commission of other crimes. Due to their methods of operation, their victims are likely to be strangers, and the offenders are more likely to use weapons and inflict harm on their target.

Many researchers have attempted to provide more specific and concise typologies for juvenile sex offenders to better understand their characteristics and the risks/needs of this particular population. O'Brien and Bera (1986) presented the most in-depth typological system associated with the peer/adult offenders, which included seven categories: naïve experimenters, under socialized child exploiters, sexual aggressives, sexual compulsives, group influenced offenders, and pseudosocialized. **Naïve experimenters** are young, have minimal social skills, lack sexual experiences, and the offenses are typically situational. **Under-socialized child exploiters** are loners who come from dysfunctional homes, but tend to have no history of delinquent behavior. Additionally, these types of juvenile sex offenders are extremely insecure and struggle with poor self-image issues. **Sexual aggressives** are most likely to use force and violence during the sexual offense. They have a history of delinquent behavior and substance abuse or addiction, a high level of impulsivity, come from a violent home environment, and typically prey on peers and adults. **Sexual compulsives** are those who have deviant sexual fantasies that turn into compulsion. These juveniles are normally quiet and anxious, come from extremely strict homes, and may exhibit paraphilic tendencies. **Paraphilia** is considered an intense sexual arousal to atypical objects, people, and situations. This can include sexual interests in children, animals, sexual sadism, and exhibitionism. **Disturbed impulsive** offenders lack impulse control and often have psychological disorders, while **group influenced offenders** commit sexually natured crimes to impress their peer groups. Lastly, **pseudosocialized** juveniles are narcissistic, have superficial relationships with peers, intimacy deficits, and a high level of intelligence. Other researchers have come up with additional typologies which include such categories as child molesters, rapists, sexually reactive, fondlers, paraphiliac offenders and an "other" category for those who do not fit any one typology.

2.5.5 Cyber Offenders

With the advent of the internet, sexual abuse against children has rapidly increased over the past few decades. There are three types of cyber crimes related to sex offenses. These crimes include taking pornographic images of children and making them accessible via the internet, sending children pornographic images, and soliciting and luring children online. While many laws have been put into place to protect children from such predators, it is difficult to identify and control such crimes due to the anonymity and exponential evolution associated with the internet.

Those who commit their sex offenses via the computer can be classified in several ways: first, by their cyber actions, such as viewing pornography or soliciting prospective victims; second, by the frequency with which they view and/or send child pornography; and lastly, by the age the perpetrators choose to seek. McLaughlin (1998) examined cyber offenders and established that many retain occupations that indirectly provide them access to children, such as teachers, clergy, photographers, building superintendents, law enforcement officers, social workers, and medical personnel. Additionally, McLaughlin established typologies of cyber offenders that include: collectors, manufacturers, travelers, and chatters. Table 2.2 provides descriptions of these typologies.

2.6 VICTIM CHARACTERISTICS

Sex offenders typically choose individuals with whom they have easy access. Just as in the case studies discussed at the beginning of the chapter, victims may include a teacher's student, a pastor's church member, or an intoxicated acquaintance. These are instances wherein the offender had easy access to the victim. They are also cases wherein the offender could easily be seen with the victim without it raising too

Table 2.2 Typology of Cyber Sex Offenders	
Typology	**Characteristics**
Collectors	Collects and trades pictures of children
	Seeks out children according to specific characteristics (age, gender, race, build)
	Normally single and socially isolated
	Hold occupations which allow for easy access to children
Travelers	Chat online and solicit meetings with victims
	Victims are usually adolescents
	Typically "groom" their victims—paying them to meet
	May collect pornography
	Usually fits a fixated typology
Manufacturers	Make child pornography
	May take photos in public place or own children and post them on the internet
	Many sexual abuse children and have a history of past offenses
Chatters	May collect child "erotica" instead of pornography
	Engages in "cyber sex"
	Attempts to instill trust in victims
	Typically escalates to talking on phone and then meeting in person
McLaughlin 1998	

many suspicions among outside observers. Sex offenders also typically prey on the most vulnerable individuals, whether they are adults or children. For example, in the case of the pastor, he was able to take his position as a minister and abuse a troubled teen. Additionally, they search for victims who may be alone, who are trusting, and who may appear weak. No matter whom perpetrators choose as their victim, most often they choose to victimize someone they know. According to the Bureau of Justice Statistics, females who are 34 and younger and live in lower socioeconomic and rural areas are more susceptible to sexual assault. Over 78% of sexual violence cases between 1995 and 2010 involved an offender who was a family member, intimate partner, friend, or acquaintance (Bureau of Justice Statistics).

Depending on the typology of the offender, they may fixate on a particular gender, age, body type, or hair and eye color. According to reports, Ted Bundy preyed on women who looked very similar to his ex-girlfriend. He focused his attention on younger women of a slender build with long dark hair and brown eyes. The Atlanta murders involved a man whose victims were all African American juvenile males.

2.7 CONCLUSION

In sum, we provided a general description of sex offender characteristics, focusing on their social, psychological, and contextual backgrounds. Sex offenders are not considered a homogeneous group; however, researchers have attempted to classify them according to typologies. In addition, we provided a general discussion of offender motivations, victim characteristics, and offender selection processes. Understanding these aspects can be paramount in the process of offender identification and the prevention of sex crimes.

REFERENCES

Guttmacher, M., & Weihofen, H. (1952). Sex offenses journal of criminal law. *Criminology & Police Science, 43*, 153–175.

Kopp (1962).

Gebhard, Gagnon, Pomeroy, & Christenson (1965). *Sex offenders: an analysis of types.* Harper & Row.

Berger, R. D. (2000). *Successfully investigating acquaintance sex assault.* National Center for Women and Policing: OJP.

Robertiello and Terry, 2007.

Groth, N. (1978). *Men who rape: the psychology of the offender.* New York: Plenum Press.

Freund, K. (1990). Courtship disorder. In W. L. Marshall, D. R. Laws, & H. E. Barbaree (Eds.), *Handbook of sexual assault: issues, theories and treatment of the offender.* New York: Plenum Press.

Knight, & Prentkey (1990). Classifying sexual offenders: the development and corroboration of taxonomic models. In Marshall, Laws, & Barbaree (Eds.), *Handbook of sexual assault: issues, theories, and treatment of the offender.* New York: Plenum Press, Chapter 3.

Terry, K., & Tallon, J. (2004). Child sexual abuse: A review of the literature. The Nature and Scope of the Problem of Sexual Abuse of Minors by Priests and Deacons, 1950–2002. Washington, D.C.: United States Conference of Catholic Bishops.

Terry, & Tallon (2004). Can we profile sex offenders?: A review of sex offender typologies. *Aggression and Violent Behaviour, 12*(5), 508–518.

O' Brien, & Bera (1986). Adolescent sexual offenders: a descriptive typology. *Preventing Sexual Abuse: A Newsletter of the National Family Life Education Network, 1*, 2–4.

McLaughlin, J. (1998). Technophilia: A modern day paraphilia. *Knight stick: Publication of the New Hampshire police association, Vol. 51*, 47–51 Spring/Summer.

CHAPTER 3

Crime Scene Investigation

3.1 CASE STUDY

Sunday, January 5, 1997, at 5:00 a.m., a 34-year-old black female was using a pay phone on the 6300 block of Hil-Mar Drive in Forestville, Maryland, a suburb located in the southeast region of the Washington, D.C. metropolitan area. The phone booth was near a gas station directly across from a small shopping mall on a busy street lined with large apartment complexes. A black male with a chipped or missing tooth approached the woman, riding a bicycle and wearing a green camouflage coat and a black ski mask. The woman was crying, and the man, whom she had seen in the area earlier, offered to let her use his home phone. The woman accompanied the man to a complex on Hil-Mar Drive, where he claimed his apartment was located. They entered an apartment that turned out to be vacant, where the man produced a handgun and raped the woman. (M.O., Suspect Description)

Wednesday, February 19, 1997, at 12:46 a.m., a 25-year-old black female was walking home from her job at a fast food restaurant in Forestville, Maryland. Her route followed Marlboro Pike, a road with a high volume of vehicle and pedestrian traffic that took her past a high school campus located across from a wooded area. As she reached the school, a black male she had seen in the area earlier, riding a black ten-speed bicycle, approached the woman. He was approximately 25 years old, five feet seven inches tall, and weighed 150 pounds. The man had a chipped or missing tooth and was wearing tan boots, blue or black sweat-pants, a black ski mask, and a green camouflage coat. He struck up a conversation with the woman, then drew a gun and forced her into the wooded area, raped her, then left the scene on his bicycle. The attacker's DNA was collected from the victim's rape kit. (DNA match)

Monday, November 20, 2000, at 6:00 p.m., a 35-year-old white female was walking into her townhouse community located in Alexandria, Virginia. A black male approached her, approximately five feet ten inches tall, wearing a black ski cap, t-shirt, and blue cargo pants. He asked for directions, and as she began to answer, he pulled out a knife, placed the woman in a headlock, and forced her behind a row of townhouses. He attempted to rob and rape her, but the woman, who was in the military, wrestled the knife from the suspect, and he fled. Investigators were able to lift the suspect's DNA from skin cells left on the blade of the knife. (DNA)

Friday, December 28, 2001, at 7:30 p.m., a 29-year-old black female was waiting at a bus stop next to a wooded area in Alexandria, Virginia, near a busy intersection surrounded by apartment complexes. A black male smoking a cigarette approached her and asked the victim when the next bus would arrive and, as she attempted to answer, the five foot eight inch, one-hundred-eighty pound man pulled out a knife and forced the woman into an apartment complex across the street. He led her behind a large electrical box hidden by shrubs and attempted to rob her, stating he knew she must have money because she "works all the time." He then told the woman to remove one shoe and a leg from her pants. He told the woman to "stop shaking" and pulled her clothes over her face as he raped her. The suspect's DNA was collected from evidence collected in the victim's rape kit. (DNA)

Saturday, January 28, 2006, at 2:21 a.m., a 46-year-old black female was in her multi-family home in New Haven, Connecticut, a run-down community known for drug trafficking and prostitution. A black male wearing leather gloves and speaking with a Caribbean accent entered the home through an unlocked door that opened onto a back porch. Before entering the home, the suspect defecated on the porch and trailed feces inside as he entered the victim's home. He threatened her by telling her he had an accomplice in the upstairs bedroom with her 15-year-old daughter. He then demanded the woman "stop shaking" and covered her face with a bed sheet while he raped her. As he left the scene, the attacker stole twenty-four dollars cash and took the victim's mobile phones. (M.O.)

Wednesday, January 10, 2007, at 1:21 a.m., a 27-year-old female was asleep in the bedroom of her first floor apartment located in New Haven, Connecticut. She awoke to find a black male who had entered the residence through an unlocked window in the bedroom. He wore a knit cap and spoke with an accent when he threatened to kill the woman's eleven-month-old son, who was sleeping in a crib in the same room. He placed a pillowcase over the victim's head and raped her. After raping her, he asked the victim if she "liked it," then scolded her for not locking her windows with a baby in the apartment. A rape kit produced a DNA sample from the attacker. (DNA)

Friday, October 31, 2009, at 9:11 p.m., three young black females were walking home after trick-or-treating in the Washington, D.C. suburb of Woodbridge, Virginia. As the girls passed through a strip mall and a 24-hour drugstore, they were approached from behind by a black male in his forties, wearing a black ski mask and brandishing a handgun. The man, speaking through clenched teeth, forced the three girls into a secluded wooded area. As he raped the two older victims, the third victim used her mobile phone to call for help, detailing their location. The youngest girl's mother rushed to the scene, approaching the wooded area from one side as police lights and sirens approached from the other. The assailant fled through the trees and was not apprehended by the police; however, DNA samples were collected from the rape victims.

3.2 SOURCE: WASHINGTON POST

Local law enforcement investigators started to notice patterns in these attacks and soon realized they were dealing with a serial rapist. The offender came to be known by law enforcement and the public as the East Coast Rapist. Diligent collection and documentation of evidence began to tie together crimes that were committed across jurisdictional lines in four states: Maryland, Virginia, Connecticut, and Rhode Island. The geographical proximity of the attacks led investigators to believe the rapist was a truck driver. Furthermore, DNA collected at the scenes conclusively connected 12 of the 17 attacks to a single offender. Although DNA evidence identified a single offender for many of the cases, investigators were unable to connect the DNA to a particular individual. About 5 of the 17 cases did not provide DNA evidence, but were related to the other cases through similarities in modi operandi, geography, and suspect descriptions. Investigators culled through thousands of leads and collected DNA from potential suspects, eliminating more than 700 individuals.

In December, 2009, authorities announced the formation of the East Coast Rape Task Force, a multijurisdictional investigative force that would include law enforcement representatives from:

- Fairfax County, Virginia
- Prince William County, Virginia
- Prince George's County, Maryland
- Town of Leesburg, Virginia
- New Haven, Connecticut
- Cranston, Rhode Island
- Federal Bureau of Investigation
- United States Marshals Service

It was the consensus of the task force members that catching the East Coast Rapist would require more than just strong collaboration between police agencies, but would also require the assistance of the media and the public. The task force launched the web site www.east-coastrapist.com, which provided details of the attacks and composite sketches of the suspect, and provided a means for the public to provide information to authorities. The suspicion that the suspect was a truck driver led the task force to utilize alternative methods of public exposure. The FBI collaborated with a billboard advertising company who allowed the task force to post information, including sketches of the suspect, on electronic billboards along the I-95 corridor from Maine to Virginia. The task force also launched an aggressive television news campaign on local and national networks.

Figure 3.1 Sketches of suspect.

Figure 3.2 Billboard post of suspect sketch.

On February 28, 2011 the investigative techniques employed by the task force paid off when a tip was received by Prince George's County Police implicating Aaron H. Thomas, a name that had appeared on a short list of suspects as being the East Coast Rapist. The caller, an acquaintance of Thomas, provided investigators with unreleased details that further solidified Thomas as a probable suspect. The task force immediately searched records in the database that verified Thomas was residing in New Haven, Connecticut. On Thursday, March 3, 2011, New Haven investigators tracked Aaron Thomas to a court appearance for an unrelated larceny charge and observed him smoking a cigarette during a break in court proceedings. They collected the discarded cigarette butt, along with the saliva contained in the filter and delivered the evidence to the Connecticut State Forensic Science Lab for analysis. The following morning, Friday, March 4, 2011, the lab confirmed that, after fourteen years of investigation and careful collection and documentation of evidence in the case, the DNA taken from the cigarette butt was a match to the East Coast Rapist.

That same afternoon, 39-year-old Aaron H. Thomas was arrested by the U.S. Marshals Fugitive Task Force at his home in New Haven, Connecticut. The charges of two counts of rape, three counts of abduction, and three counts of use of a firearm in the commission of a felony stemmed from his Halloween attack on three teenage girls in Woodbridge, Virginia. One of the prosecutors at Thomas' arraignment hearing stated the suspect asked in court, "Why haven't you picked me up sooner?"

Figure 3.3 Aaron Thomas mug shot.

3.3 CRIME SCENE INVESTIGATION

Popular television shows such as CSI and NCIS have become popular over the last several years. These shows portray a criminal justice system in which investigators play the role of detective, cop, crime scene investigator, forensic scientist, and medical examiner. They solve crimes in a one-hour show wherein the perpetrator is inevitably found, interrogated, arrested, and convicted. While these television programs are entertaining, they do not reveal the realities of the criminal justice system. During an investigation, many actors play a role—from the responding officers to the crime scene technicians, to the investigators, to medical personnel. All of these individuals have special jobs, which assist in a process of catching the "bad guy"—which always takes longer than an episode of CSI.

Forensic science can be defined as the utilization of science in conjunction with the law. In criminal cases, forensic scientists are often involved in the search for and examination of physical traces, which might be useful for establishing or excluding connections between suspects, crime scenes, and/or victims.

3.4 HISTORY

The earliest forensic investigators were medical men who were typically the first to arrive at the scene of a death (Nickell and Fischer, 1999). The Chinese book entitled His Duan Yu "The Washing Away of Wrongs" (Saferstein, 1995 and Nickel & Fisher, 2000) was the earliest record of physicians using medical knowledge to solve crimes. While this book contained unscientific information regarding crime, it assisted in establishing some basic medical procedures, such as determining if an individual was drowned by examining the victim's lungs for water or focusing on pressure marks on the throat and cartilage damage to the neck to identify death by strangulation.

Over the years, crime scene investigations have slowly evolved with technological advancements. In 1860, a prison warden named Stevens made the first scientific attempt at criminal identification. He took measurements of criminals' heads, feet, ears, and the length of their bodies. This method was soon abandoned and replaced with a more elaborate form of anthropometry (the science of measuring the body) by Frenchman **Alphonse Bertillion** in 1879. By 1882 this method, referred to as *bertillonage*, was routinely used to identify criminals through the measurements and tabulations of factors such as height, arm length, head circumference, length of the right ear, and various other measurements and photographs. Eventually, this process was replaced with what is commonly in use today: fingerprints (Nickell & Fischer, 2000).

Although several individuals contributed to the science of fingerprint identification, **Francis Galton** is recognized as the first person to scientifically study fingerprints. He is most recognized for a system of classifying fingerprints for filing purposes. His 1892 publication entitled *Finger Prints* provided the first statistical evidence supporting the uniqueness of fingerprints. Additionally, this publication described the fundamental principles that continue to be utilized as a method of fingerprint identification today (Saferstein, 1995).

3.4.1 Locard's exchange principle

Edmond Locard was a French criminalist known for being a pioneer in forensic science and criminology, often informally referred to as the "Sherlock Holmes of France," Edmond Locard is perhaps most well known for his formulation of **Locard's Exchange Principle**, a theory relating to the transfer of trace evidence between objects. The principle states that "every contact leaves a trace;" therefore, any two objects that come into contact with one another will each take something from the other object or leave something behind. It is therefore not possible to come into contact with an element without changing it in some small way, either by adding to the environment or taking something away from the environment. This principle is vital to criminal investigations because it can link suspects to victims and/or locations. It is physical evidence of contact, though often times miniscule, that has the potential to become a key factor in a criminal investigation.

3.5 INVESTIGATION AND EVIDENCE

Due to the fact that the victims in sexual assault cases are often viewed by law enforcement and the courts with a degree of mistrust, a sound sexual assault case relies heavily on evidence acquired through law enforcement, crime scene technicians, and medical staff. Unlike other crimes such as homicide or robbery, the responding officer is required to play a much greater part in evidence collection and preservation. In a murder investigation the first officer who arrives on the scene is often only responsible for securing, the crime scene until detectives and crime scene investigators arrive. In sexual assault cases, however, the responding officer is expected to ensure that all physical evidence, that may be lost by the victim or during a medical examination, be collected and preserved properly to ensure its use for scientific examination and comparison during the investigation process.

If an assault is reported by phone to law enforcement or emergency services, the individual receiving the information (dispatcher, emergency services) must determine the facts and whether the victim is currently in danger to initiate the appropriate response. They must dispatch law enforcement assistance promptly. In addition to victim information, the individual receiving the report must try to obtain offender location, existence of a weapon, and any and all necessary identifying information. Whenever possible, the victim should be kept on the telephone until a first responding officer arrives to minimize the possibility of loss of evidence.

The **responding officer** has the responsibility of ensuring victims' safety, securing the surrounding area (i.e., crime scene), and preserving any and all evidence associated with the crime. The first officer on the scene must, therefore, be knowledgeable in securing the crime scene, preserving evidence, and assisting the victim. The officer must also be a skilled interviewer to elicit details of the assault from the victim and then, from these details, deduce what evidence is likely to be available (Fisher, 2000).

After the victim has provided details of the sexual assault, it is necessary to obtain a detailed description of the offender. In cases when the offender is unknown, a detailed description is essential for identifying suspects. It can also be used in different ways: to link to other cases, prioritize suspects, develop interrogation strategies, and form an investigative plan. For a known or recognized offender, victims are asked to provide identifying information about the offender such as name, address, phone number, work, routines, friends, etc. For known offenders, detailed physical descriptions are also important. For example, investigators should ask the victim about characteristics related to the assailant's hair color, eyes, nose, mouth, etc. (see Table 3.1).

After questions have been asked concerning the assailant, it is paramount to ask additional questions that may lead to individuals who witnessed the crime. Law enforcement may ask victims if there were any loud noises during the assault such as screams, furniture or large items knocked to the floor, doors slammed, etc. Further, they will determine whether the victim is aware of any witnesses who may have seen or heard the offender make the initial contact with the victim, use physical restraint or force, and/or exit the crime scene (Jurkanin T. J., 1996).

As an investigator in a sexual assault case, it is important to remember it is not unusual for a victim's statement to include discrepancies and inconsistencies. The circumstances of the sexual assault can cause a victim to be disorganized and confused when attempting to relay the information to law enforcement. Investigators must resist making any assumptions about the validity of any statements until the victim has an opportunity to finish the initial account of the assault. If there are inconsistencies in the victim's statement, the investigator must delicately explain the inconsistencies to the victim. It is important to

Table 3.1 Assailant Characteristic	
Hair	Color, style, texture, amount (thinning, thick, bald)
Eyes	Color, size, unusual characteristics (crossed, etc.) glasses (kind, style), eyebrows (bushy, thin)
Nose	Size, flat, broken, pointed, thick.
Mouth	Lips (thin, full, shape), moustache (color, thin, thick, type), beard (color, full, thin, thick, type)
Teeth	Crooked, spaces, braces, missing, gold, broken, discolored
Voice	Accent, speech impediment, harsh, refined, pitch, soft, loud, words spoken during assault
Breath	Odor (foul, sweet), alcohol, smoke, garlic
Body	Type (thin, fat, muscular), scars, defining marks (tattoos, moles, birthmarks), odor (cologne, body odor, etc.), method(s) used to restrain or strike victim (hands, body parts)
Height	Range (compared to interviewer)
Weight	Range (compared to interviewer)
Jewelry	Rings, earrings, nipple rings, nose rings, watch, bracelet, necklace, etc.
Clothing	Brand, color, markings, drawings, shoes (clean/new, dirty/ old) work clothes, sweats

***Document the comparisons used for any height, weight or other range comparisons. The documentation of these comparisons will assist in explaining any later discrepancies that may arise.

remain nonjudgmental—the investigator may not have initially understood the victim correctly, and should explore the basis for the inconsistency. The investigator can request the victim to make sense of the inconsistent details, but should not ask the victim to justify a particular behavior or statement (e.g., why the victim was drinking, or the why victim got into a car with a stranger). Risk-taking behaviors may be the subject of the inconsistent statements. The officer will take into account it is not unusual for victims to omit risk-taking behaviors out of fear such behaviors will be viewed negatively. The officer will need to encourage clarity in this area, because the credibility of the victim will be enhanced if the behaviors are identified and addressed early in the investigation.

Crime scene investigators offer vital assistance to the police in sexual assault investigations. Crime scene investigators and/or other officers who collect evidence have multiple duties when assessing a crime scene. They use various types of equipment, develop, secure, and package physical evidence for scientific evaluation and comparison, prepare detailed reports on the observations and activities at the scene, and testify in court regarding the findings, handling, and processing methods used at the crime scene. Additionally, they must determine available facts of the case by interviewing the appropriate responding and

Table 3.2 Evidence Collection Checklist
• Assess the crime scene for physical evidence, including fingerprints, body fluids, footprints, disturbed or disrupted objects, or furniture.
• Photograph or videotape the crime scene before touching, moving, or disrupting potential evidence.
• Conduct a comprehensive, non-destructive search for all available physical evidence.
• Photograph each item as it originally appeared at the crime scene prior to collection of evidence. Provide an indication of size or scale if appropriate.
• Collect, properly package, and mark evidence from the crime scene. Note: Air dry evidence before packaging to avoid deterioration of specimen. This is essential for a blood sample to be used for DNA testing
• Complete the necessary documents to transfer evidence to the proper crime lab for processing.
• Contact the investigating agency with preliminary results of crime scene analysis and request follow-up information.
• Transport those items of evidence requiring laboratory analysis to the proper crime lab.
• Store remaining items of evidence in a secure storage area to properly maintain the chain of custody.
• At the hospital, with the victim's consent, photograph injuries on the victim, or arrange for same sex medical personnel to do so. Re-photograph the victim as the injuries change appearance.
• Finish the final sketch of the scene.
• Complete the final report.

investigating officer(s), as well as examining the evidence collection checklist. An example of a checklist is found in Table 3.2.

Trace evidence is any type of materials left at, or taken from, a crime scene. This may include evidence acquired through contact between two surfaces, such as shoes and soil or upholstery transferred by kneeling on a rug or sitting on a chair. **Class Characteristics** are physical qualities shared by a group of similar items. **Individual Characteristics** are physical qualities that are unique to an individual item. All physical objects have both class and individual characteristics (Nickell & Fischer 1999).

Blood and body fluid evidence are typically stored in paper bags and must be dried completely under natural conditions before packaging. While protocol for collecting evidence may vary across states and/ or departments, blood and body fluid evidence is usually placed in a box, paper packet, or envelope with a label of the specimen description on the outside of the package. Along with the description of the specimen, the date it was secured, the investigator or crime scene technician's initials, the case name and number, and where the specimen was retrieved (located at the crime scene) is recorded on the packaging label. Whenever the evidence exchanges hands, either from crime scene investigator to crime lab or from the hospital (in the case of a rape kit) to law enforcement, initials are labeled on the package to ensure a proper record of the chain of custody.

3.6 VICTIM

After a sexual assault occurs, the victim often feels physically and psychologically dirty. They may have an overwhelming desire to bathe, wash, throw away clothing, and clean up the crime scene. During the interview process, investigators must determine if any or all of these actions took place before they arrived. If so, collecting items such as washcloths or tissues may be be neccessary to obtain evidence. These items may contain small amounts of semen from the perpetrator. The victim should make every effort to preserve any and all evidence associated with the perpetrator. They should not shower or use the restroom. They should not change their clothing, comb their hair, or attempt to clean up the crime scene. Moving or touching anything the offender may have physically contacted is likely to contaminate the evidence.

Investigators should also ask the victim about the patterns and actions of the perpetrator. Did the perpetrator practice any unusual acts such as urination, defecation, or oral sex? Did the perpetrator do or say anything unusual? (Jurkanin T.J. 1996).

3.7 DNA

DNA (Deoxyribonucleic acid) is the fundamental building block for an individual's entire genetic makeup, and has become an increasingly powerful tool for solving sex crimes over the past several years (Bureau of Justice Statistics www.bjs.gov 6/16/13). DNA is a powerful tool for law enforcement investigations because each person's DNA is different from another person (except for identical twins). DNA can be extracted from a number of sources such as hair, bone, teeth, saliva, and blood. As early as the 1980s, states began enacting laws that required the collection of DNA samples from offenders convicted of sexual and/or other violent crimes. The samples were then analyzed and their profiles entered into state databases. During this time, the Federal Bureau of Investigation (FBI) Laboratory assembled a working group of federal, state, and local forensic scientists to establish guidelines for the use of forensic DNA analysis in laboratories. The group proposed guidelines national quality assurance standards, and urged the creation of a national DNA database. The criminal justice community began to utilize DNA analyses more often in criminal investigations and trials; and in 1994, Congress enacted legislation to authorize the creation of a national DNA database.

In cases when a suspect is known, a sample of the person's DNA can be compared to biological evidence found at a crime scene. The results may help establish whether the suspect was at the crime scene or whether he or she committed the crime. In cases when a suspect is not known, biological evidence from the crime scene can be analyzed and compared to offender profiles contained in existing DNA databases to assist in identifying the perpetrator.

3.8 RAPE KITS AND DNA

Medical personnel are significant to the criminal justice team as the primary medical care providers and collectors of evidence. A forensic medical exam is often performed at a hospital or local health care facility. Victims should be immediately examined by a sexual assault nurse (SANE), sexual assault forensic examiner (SAFE), or another trained forensic medical professional. The forensic exam usually takes between three to four hours to perform. The extensive amount of time dedicated to this procedure is due to the need for special attention to the victim. This process ensures the victim is medically safe and protected. Additionally, it is important to provide an extensive examination to properly collect any and all possible evidence so investigators may access the evidence acquired through the forensic medical exam.

Medical professionals begin the examination by first writing a detailed history of the victim. This reveals a picture of the health status of the victim, including any and all medications consumed, as well as any pre-existing conditions that may not be associated with the assault. Before, during, and after the medical examination, medical personnel should interview the victim. The method by which the interviews are conducted may affect the investigation. Sensitive treatment by medical personnel can help engage the victim in the investigative process. Law enforcement officers should work with hospital personnel to ensure the victim is not further traumatized during the examination process. Following the initial medical interview, an extensive examination of the entire body will occur. This includes an external and internal examination. A collection of blood, urine, hair, and any other body secretion samples is usually taken. Additionally, the medical examiners take photographic documentation of the assault such as bruises, cuts, and scrapes. During this time all clothing (especially undergarments) from the victim is collected. While a police officer may not be present during the evidence collection process of the medical examination, police must know what will be collected through the use of evidence collection kits, and be able to suggest to hospital personnel what other evidence may be important to collect from the victim. After this process is complete, the medical professional will explain the various treatments for sexually transmitted infections the victim may have been exposed to during the assault (Jurkanin T.J.).

The sexual assault forensic exam kit (often referred to as a rape kit) allows for the collection of DNA, along with any other forensic evidence associated with a sexual assault. The rape kit is generally a large envelope or cardboard box that typically includes instructions, bags and sheets for evidence collection, swabs, combs, envelopes for hairs and fibers, blood collection devices, and documentation forms. Once the evidence has been collected, the kit stays with the SANE or medical provider until law enforcement personnel or the crime lab picks it up. It is paramount the hospital and police agree on how the chain of custody for the evidence will be maintained and how evidence will be transferred from the hospital to the police.

According to the Violence Against Women and the Department of Justice Reauthorization Act of 2005, states must ensure the victim has access to free or full reimbursement of all medical treatment involved in the forensic medical examination, even if the victim chooses not to cooperate with law enforcement officials. Prior to this 2005 Act, states were required to provide free medical exams, but could put various conditions on the free treatment, such as cooperating with investigators. This law allows time for victims to decide if they want to press charges against their attacker. Since a sexual assault is extremely traumatic, some victims are unable to make legal decisions immediately following their experience. This law allows the victim time to make a decision while preserving evidence that would otherwise be lost. In cases when the victim is initially unsure about pursuing a case, a "Jane Doe Rape Kit" may be used. This allows a victim to have forensic evidence collected while maintaining anonymity and privacy. In some states, victims are provided with a code number they can utilize to identify themselves if they choose to report the crime at a later date.

Once the rape kit is complete and stored, states have varying time frames in which the kit may be retained; therefore, the victim must be aware of how long the kit will be retained along with the disposal time of the kit. If the victim chooses to proceed with reporting the crime, the evidence is typically examined and processed at a local crime lab. Processing collected evidence may take only a few weeks; however, many crime labs throughout the country have significant backlogs. Due to these backlogs, the wait time for tested evidence may range from a few weeks to a couple of months or longer.

3.9 EVIDENCE COLLECTION—SUSPECT

When an arrest is made or a suspect is identified, the suspect's clothing will be collected, marked, and packaged for transfer to a crime lab. Photographs will be taken of the individual. The consent of the suspect, a search warrant, or a court order is required to collect biological evidence from the suspect. Biological evidence will also be collected from the suspect, which may include mouth swabs (saliva) or hair samples, which assist in the comparison of any DNA acquired at the scene or on the victim. A search warrant may be obtained to search the suspect's residence, vehicle, or place of employment for items which may have been taken from the victim or the crime scene, or any evidence that may have been transferred to the victim or crime scene from the defendant.

3.10 DATABASES

Known as the lifeline of law enforcement, the **National Crime Information Center** (NCIC) is an electronic clearinghouse of crime data that can be utilized by virtually every criminal justice agency nationwide, 24 hours a day, 365 days a year. NCIC was launched on January 27, 1967 with five files and 356,784 records. By the end of 2011, NCIC contained 11.7 million records in 19 files. During 2011, NCIC averaged 7.9 million transactions daily. NCIC assists criminal justice professionals in the apprehension of fugitives, locating missing persons, recovering stolen property, and identifying terrorists. It also assists law enforcement officers in performing their official duties more safely, and provides information necessary to protect the public.

Currently, the NCIC database consists of 21 files. There are seven property files containing records of stolen articles, boats, guns, license plates, parts, securities, and vehicles. There are 14 persons files, including: Supervised Release; National Sex Offender Registry; Foreign Fugitive; Immigration Violator; Missing Person; Protection Order;

Unidentified Person; U.S. Secret Service Protective; Gang; Known or Appropriately Suspected Terrorist; Wanted Person; Identity Theft; Violent Person; and National Instant Criminal Background Check System (NICS) Denied Transaction (FBI.gov).

CODIS stands for combined DNA index system. This system houses information regarding DNA evidence in a database to make comparisons locally as well as nationally. Through the use of this type of system, biological evidence found at one crime scene can be connected to other crime scenes, linking them to the same perpetrator. A forensic laboratory receives evidence in a criminal investigation and is asked to perform DNA testing on that evidence. The evidence may be part of a rape case or a homicide. The DNA profile obtained from the crime scene evidence is called a forensic unknown. The laboratory know whose profile it is, but they know it is associated with a crime. The laboratory enters that profile into CODIS. If it is a local case, the profile is entered into the local CODIS system and uploaded to the state level. At the state level, the profile will be compared with all the offenders from the state's database. The forensic unknown may or may not match with other DNA records at the state level. On a weekly basis, the state uploads its DNA records to NDIS, the national level database. Then the profile is compared against all 50 states' offender profiles to see if there is a match. If there is, the CODIS software automatically returns messages in the system to the laboratories involved. The local labs evaluate the matches and release that information to the law enforcement agency. That is how a previously unknown DNA profile is associated with a known offender.

Another database often used by law enforcement agencies is **AFIS** (Automated Fingerprint Identification System). This system houses fingerprints from individuals who have been arrested for a crime. The proper collection and identification of fingerprints is crucial to the identification of a perpetrator. Petersilia (1975, p. 12) describes the importance of fingerprint analysis:

> *No matter how competent the evidence technician is at performing his job, the gathering of physical evidence at a crime scene will be futile unless such evidence can be properly processed and analyzed. Since fingerprints are by far the most frequently retrieved physical evidence, making the system of analyzing such prints effective will contribute the most toward greater success in identifying criminal offenders through the use of physical evidence.*

Before this database was established, note cards carrying fingerprints were sorted, maintained, and compared by cadres and clerks. AFIS was established to provide a system wherein fingerprints could be housed and compared easily through the computerized system. This system uses digital imaging to capture a fingerprint, which then can be compared to a database of fingerprint records to determine the identity of an individual. This system uses individual characteristics of each fingerprint to make comparisons and find similar fingerprints within the database.

The Federal Bureau of Investigation established an extension of AFIS in 1999. **IAFIS** (Integrated Automated Fingerprint Identification System) is a national fingerprint and criminal history system that responds to requests 24 hours a day, 365 days a year to assist local, state, and federal partners in solving and preventing crime. IAFIS provides automated fingerprint search, latent search, electronic image storage, and electronic exchange of fingerprints and responses. IAFIS not only carries information pertaining to fingerprints, but also criminal histories; mug shots; scars and tattoo photos; physical characteristics like height, weight, and hair and eye color; and aliases. The database not only carries information regarding criminals, but it also carries civil fingerprints of individuals in the military and federal employees.

IAFIS is the largest biometric database in the world, housing the fingerprints and criminal histories for more than 70 million subjects in the criminal master file, along with more than 34 million civil prints. The average response time for an electronic criminal fingerprint submission is about 27 minutes. Electronic civil submissions are processed in around an hour. IAFIS processed more than 61 million fingerprint submissions in 2010.

3.11 LInX

The Law Enforcement Information Exchange, or LInX, was initiated in 2003 in response to the 9/11 terrorists attacks. It is a regional information sharing system created, coordinated, and funded by the U.S. Naval Criminal Investigative Service (NCIS). LInX breaks down artificial jurisdictional and technical barriers between municipal, county, state, and federal law enforcement agencies, providing information quickly across jurisdictional lines. This state-of-the-art collaborative information sharing program is currently operating in 11 regional locations around the United States. Data from arrest and incident records, investigations, traffic reports, computer-aided dispatch data, booking records, warrants, field interviews, and other key law enforcement data sources are easily and quickly accessible through this database (FBI.gov).

3.12 ROLE OF THE CRIME LAB

Crime laboratories are an integral part of law enforcement's response to sexual assault. Crime labs provide detailed information and training on proper collection, packaging, and handling of information. The services and abilities of the labs define what evidence can be analyzed for use in the prosecution of a sex offender. Police officers and investigators should be aware of the range of services offered by the lab that serves the area for which the department is responsible. Typically, forensic crime laboratories are prepared to respond to requests for a variety of forensic services, such as DNA analysis, controlled substance identification, latent fingerprint examination, and questioned documents and ballistic identification (Bureau of Justice Statistics www.bjs.gov 6/16/13).

REFERENCES

Petersilia, J. (1975). *The collection and processing of physical evidence; WN-9062 – DOJ*. Santa Monica, CA: RAND Corporation.

Jurkanin, T. J. (1996). Model Guidelines and Sex Crimes Investigation Manual for Illinois Law Enforcement.

Nickell, J., & Fisher, J. (1999). *Crime Science: Methods of Forensic Detection.* Lexington, Kentucky: University Press of Kentucky.

Petersilia, J. (1975). *The collection and processing of physical evidence; WN-9062 _ DOJ*. Santa Monica, CA: RAND Corporation.

Bureau of Justice Statistics. < www.bjs.gov >.

Federal Bureau of Investigation – fbi.gov

CHAPTER 4

Interrogation and Interviews

4.1 CASE STUDY

On Sunday, February 7, 2010, Colonel Russell Williams, a decorated commander of Canadian Forces Base Trenton, responded to a request by the Ontario Provincial Police to answer a few questions regarding the disappearance of twenty-seven-year-old Jessica Lloyd. Less than ten hours later, the rising star of the Canadian Air Force had confessed to a host of crimes and was facing 88 charges including breaking and entry, sexual assault, and murder. Between 2009 and 2010, Williams was the commander of the CFB Trenton, the largest military airbase in Canada. He was a well-respected, decorated military pilot who flew VIP aircraft for dignitaries such as Queen Elizabeth II, Prince Phillip, and the Prime Minister of Canada.

Figure 4.1 Russell Williams.

The first known break-in occurred in September 2007, when Williams entered a neighbor's home, who were out of town visiting their dying mother. He went into the 12-year-old daughter's room, photographed himself masturbating in a pair of red panties, and left with six pairs of underwear and bras. A series of 14 time-stamped photographs revealed he burglarized this neighbor's home several times after the initial break-in. A few weeks later, on November 1, 2007, Williams broke into the home of another neighbor living on the same street. He spent two hours taking photographs of himself posing on a bed, wearing panties, and a camisole.

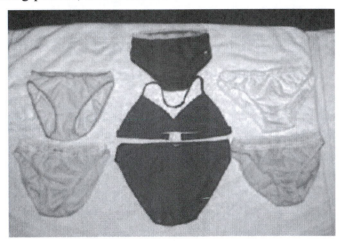

Figure 4.2 Underwear stolen from victim.

Williams targeted the homes of attractive women in their late teens to early 30s, but often photographed himself wearing undergarments belonging to young girls. On January 1, 2008, Williams photographed himself in the bedroom of a 15 year old girl stroking his erect penis with one of her makeup brushes. He then ejaculated on her dresser and left the brush behind for her to use. Other photos showed him in a room shared by 11-year-old twins, and on another occasion, he stole undergarments from the room of a twelve-year-old girl, leaving the message "merci" (French for "thank you") on her computer screen. He attempted to use personal items located in the homes to familiarize himself with the names of the victims.

Williams often entered the homes through open windows or doors, but occasionally pushed in screens or picked locks. Between

September, 2007 and November, 2009, Williams committed 82 burglaries or attempted burglaries on 48 homes in Belleville-Tweed and Ottawa, visiting one home as many as nine times. His expertise in clandestinely entering homes and rarely leaving behind any evidence accounted for 61 unreported burglaries. It was his detailed record-keeping that revealed the crimes to authorities. He kept detailed journals of his crimes, archived thousands of explicit, time-stamped photographs taken at crime scenes using a complex file folder system on computer hard drives, and kept inventories of items he took as trophies from each location. He began by photographing the bedroom, including photos of personal identification such as drivers' licenses, family photos, and diplomas. After taking photos of bras and panties, as stored by the victims, he removed them from their drawers and photographed them neatly placed on the floor or the bed. He then photographed himself modeling the garments and masturbating on the victim's bed, often showing his erect penis protruding from the panties. He occasionally photographed himself licking or kissing the panties while masturbating. Before leaving the home, Williams stole bras and panties, sex toys, or other personal items, which he stored in bags and boxes at his Ottawa residence. On two occasions, Williams had amassed such an extensive collection that he took some of the items to a vacant lot and burned them to make room for more.

An escalation in Williams' behavior pattern began at approximately 1:30 a.m. EST, July 11, 2009, when he made his sixth visit (of a total of nine visits) to a neighbor's home. He hid in the back yard for more than 30 minutes and watched the female resident undress and step into her shower. Williams then undressed, left his clothing in the yard, entered the home naked, and stole the woman's panties. Williams claimed this encounter made him want to "take bigger risks." He addressed this desire later as he hid behind another home, attempting to watch a teenage girl undress. He stripped off his own clothes and masturbated in the bushes outside the girl's window.

In September 2009, Williams' risky behaviors continued when he attacked a woman as she slept with her newborn baby nearby. He struck her repeatedly head, bounded her to a chair, and blindfolded her using pillowcases. The nude victim was fondled and photographed for two hours. Later the same month, a second victim was attacked in a similar manner. The woman awoke to find Williams holding her head down. Williams beat her in the head and used blankets to bind her to a chair and cover her head. He took time undressing her while he fondled and photographed the victim. At one point, Williams left the room and stole undergarments from the victim's bedroom, which he catalogued in his documentation of the attack. He broke into the victim's home two more times, not assaulting the victim, but photographing her bedroom and personal items, including her driver's license and insurance card.

On November 25, 2009, the body of 38-year-old Marie-France Comeau was found in her home. She had been raped and tortured before being murdered. The victim was a Corporal in the Canadian Air Force and served under the command of Colonel Russell Williams at Canadian Forces Base Trenton. She had served as a flight attendant piloted by Williams and lived near Williams' cottage in Tweed. During this time, he spent most weeks in Tweed, Ontario and weekends in Ottawa, Ontario with his wife.

On the night of January 28, 2010, 27-year-old Jessica Elizabeth Lloyd was reported missing to law enforcement when she failed to appear at work. During the investigation into Lloyd's disappearance, Ontario Provincial Police received a tip from witnesses who claimed to have seen a dark-colored SUV parked in a field adjacent to Lloyd's home on the night she went missing. Investigators located tire impressions in the snow where the witnesses described seeing the vehicle. Forensics determined the unique tread marks came from an uncommon make and model tire—a Toyo Open Country HTS. Boot prints were also located near the back door to Lloyd's home. On February 4, 2010, police set up a roadblock on Highway 37, connecting the towns of Belleville and Tweed, to gather information from motorists regarding Lloyd's disappearance. Russell Williams was stopped in the roadblock and questioned by police who observed his dark green Nissan Pathfinder was equipped with Toyo Open Country HTS tires. He was allowed to continue home, but was put under immediate police surveillance. Williams became the primary suspect in Lloyd's disappearance. On February 7, 2010, Williams responded to a police request to answer questions and was escorted to an interview room to face the Ontario Provincial Police's expert interrogator and polygraph technician.

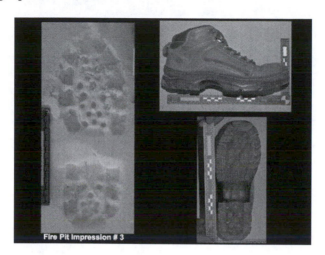

Fire Pit Impression # 3

Figure 4.3 Footwear evidence.

The interrogation room had no decor and was furnished only with a table and two chairs. Williams was offered a seat at the head of the table and the interrogator, Jim Smith, took a seat along the side of the table. Williams was advised of his rights to remain silent and to have an attorney present, which he waived. Smith began the interview by addressing Williams as "Russell." Throughout the early stages of the interview, Smith avoided addressing Williams as "Colonel," which would possibly have provided Williams with a sense of superiority. The interrogator moved close to Williams and he began the formal interview by asking, "What would you be willing to give me [...] to move past you in this investigation?" Williams responded by asking what the police needed from him. Smith informed Williams that footwear impressions had been taken from the scene of Lloyd's disappearance, and the police needed him to submit samples of his boot treads. Williams, who until that time had maintained eye contact with Smith, glanced at his shoes. Impressions were taken of his boots and submitted for immediate forensic analysis.

Figure 4.4 Williams in interrogation room.

Williams then asked Smith if the police would be discreet regarding his position at Canadian Forces Base Trenton. He expressed apprehension that rumors may circulate about his involvement in the investigation. Smith responded by explaining to Williams that discretion was the reason he had been asked to answer questions on a Sunday. Smith then asked Williams to also submit a DNA sample, to which Williams responded by shifting in his seat and releasing an audible sigh. Williams then crossed his arms and began to stare at the floor for long periods of time. He would occasionally look at Smith, but did not speak.

The boot print analysis determined the boots Williams wore to the interview matched the impressions found by the rear door to Lloyd's residence. At that point in the interrogation, Jim Smith shifted from "good cop" to "bad cop" and became more aggressive with his questioning. Smith told Williams "the issues point at you," and informed him the tire impressions found near the crime scene matched the tires of his vehicle. Williams began "buying time" by staring at the floor without speaking to the interrogator. Smith allowed the prolonged episodes of silence without interruption because he assumed Williams was analyzing the evidence against him, and weighing his ability to develop a story to refute the evidence. After one such episode, Williams looked at Smith and said, "Call me Russ, please." By this response, Smith determined he was beginning to break the militaristic resolve of his suspect.

Smith continued to refer to Williams as "Russell" as he refocused the interview to the disappearance of Jessica Lloyd. He reiterated the facts of the investigation, which suggested Williams' involvement in the case, and said that police believed Williams knew where she could be found. Williams looked up and said, "It's hard to believe this is happening." Smith responded by returning to his "good cop" persona and asked, "Russ, is there anything you want from me? [...] What are you looking for?" Smith began mirroring the movements and gestures exhibited by Williams during another period of silence. He would occasionally look up at Smith, but primarily focused his gaze at the floor, arms folded, shifting in his seat, and sighing. Approximately four hours and 40 minutes into the interrogation, Williams leaned forward and asked, "Got a map?"

Williams pinpointed the location of Jessica Lloyd's body and confessed to attacking the victim in her home on January 28, 2010. He then took the victim to his cottage in Tweed, where he spent just under 24 hours raping and torturing the victim before he killed her with a strike to the head with a heavy flashlight. During the remaining six hours of his interrogation, Williams confessed to the rape and murder of Marie-France Comeau and revealed evidence that would implicate him in 88 charges brought against him.

4.2 CONDUCTING INTERVIEWS

During a criminal investigation, **interviewing** victims, witnesses, and suspects is a vital part of the process. Investigators must be prepared to interview all types of individuals (i.e., different ages, races, and socioeconomic classes). This requires a great deal of knowledge and tact. If this process is not carried out properly, it can be detrimental to the case; therefore, investigators must be properly trained to acquire the information needed to identify and apprehend perpetrators.

The purpose of interviewing the victim is to obtain sufficient information to complete the preliminary investigation. During this time, as discussed in Chapter 3, the investigator's purpose is to acquire as much information as possible from the victim shortly following the assault. Due to the victim's emotional state the preliminary investigator may have to limit questioning in the initial interview and conduct follow-up interviews to obtain more information and address any inconsistencies in the initial interview. Guidelines for conducting successful interviews with victims include: proper setting, rapport building, interview questions and tone, and service referral.

Proper settings for interviews should be quiet and free from distraction. An investigator must make sure the victim feels secure in the location. If possible, the victim will be asked to give a statement at the police station and/or at a place of residence. The victim should be allowed to choose who is present during the interviews. If a rape crisis advocate is available, he or she may be present during the interview only if the victim signs a written waiver of confidentiality. Otherwise, the advocate should be available for the victim after the interview is concluded for any emotional or psychological support.

During the interview, it is important that the victim trusts the investigators, understands the role of the police, and has clear expectations for the investigative process. Investigators should explain the method and stages of the investigation, and the purpose of follow-up interviews. It is important that victims feel they are pertinent to the investigation process by understanding the necessity and relevance of the questions posed during the interviews and investigations. With regard to those who are conducting the interviews with victims, it is important for the investigators to remain nonjudgmental and build the victim's trust and cooperation. The attitude and conduct of investigators is important to getting the victim's story regarding the assault. An investigator who is nonjudgmental and sympathetic will put the victim at ease and should be able to acquire more information.

An interview may begin with "you" statements and questions (how are you? where would you like to conduct a statement?). The victim should then be kept informed with "we" questions ("we need to broadcast certain information to try and locate the offender") and told what is needed with "I" statements ("I need you to remember as much of the details of the offender's description as possible"). The investigator must be careful not to convey any judgment about the victim's actions prior to, during, or after the assault. Instead of asking questions such as "Did you fight back?" or "Did you try to run away?" ask instead: "What did you do next?" When questioning victims, investigators should also be mindful of the case. For example in sexual assault cases, investigators must consider the type of information that must be addressed: **consent** or **identification**.

The difference between a "consent" and "identification" case may affect the kind of investigation and evidence that will become crucial to the success or failure of the case. In consent cases, questions should focus on confrontation and the use of force. The underlying premise is to understand the context of the assault. Alternatively, identity cases require collection of information to find and apprehend offenders. This investigative process includes obtaining as much information as possible on offender characteristics, physical attributes, and other possible identifiers that will help the investigators apprehend offenders as soon as possible. Although the consent and identification investigative inquiries focus on different questions, both processes can be addressed in victim interviews and statements.

A victim's initial statement typically includes information about the crime. Investigators should not attempt to obtain detailed information regarding the sexual assault beyond the information necessary to establish an offense has occurred. More in depth information is typically acquired during follow-up interviews with the victim such as:

- Types and extent of injuries to the victim, if any
- Details of what happened
- Where the attack occurred
- Direction in which the attacker fled and by what means
- Type of weapon involved, if any
- If the attack(s) meets the elements of a sexual offense.

A good investigator will allow victims to provide information in their own words and at their own pace. They will avoid interrupting victims while they are recalling the assault. They will repeat the information using the victim's words as the interview is conducted. Further, clarifying questions may be needed to establish one or more facts. These questions might require the victim to disclose personal and embarrassing information. Good investigators will watch the victim's body language and other nonverbal responses. These cues may convey whether the victim is uncomfortable with the line of questioning. The investigators need to reassure victims their cooperation is vital to the investigation. Due to the nature of questioning, some victims may omit certain aspects of the attack in the preliminary interview due to possible discomfort. **Follow-up interviews** may be conducted to address any aspect of the interview that may have been incomplete during initial questioning. Once victims describe the assault, investigators will use the victims' vocabulary to ask clarifying questions that describe sexual acts.

When conducting interviews, the questioning may be broken down into the following: targeting, testing, threat assault, and termination. These categories allow investigators to follow a logical flow of events, starting with the initial contact, and ending with the perpetrator leaving the victim. This format eases the conversation between the investigator and victim, obtaining the most accurate and detailed account of the assault and offender.

Targeting questions are designed to establish how the offender made initial contact with the victim. The offender may be using an established pattern or method of targeting the victim.

- Where and when did the victim first observe the offender?
- What location was the victim coming from/going to?
- What was the victim doing when he/she became aware of the offender's presence?
- What was the victim thinking and feeling?
- If the offender is an acquaintance, when did the victim become aware the situation was changing and there might be a problem?
- Did the offender act in a similar manner in the past?
- Did the victim have a daily routine and if so, what routine or pattern did the victim follow when he/she was attacked?

In addition to targeting questions, investigators may also focus on **testing questions**. Before and during the attack, the offender may try to establish the vulnerability of the victim by having a brief conversation with the victim or, on the other hand, immediately become physical. Investigators will try to tap into the context prior to the attack by asking victims the following questions:

- What did the offender say to test the victim's reactions?
- Did the offender ask for directions, the time, or ask to come into the victim's home to use the phone, bathroom, or have a drink?
- What were the exact words the offender used, if possible?
- What physical testing occurred?
- Did the offender block the victim's path?
- Did the offender hold or grab the victim?
- Did the offender lock the door to the car?
- Did the offender lock the door to the residence?
- What was the victim doing during this time?
- What was the victim thinking and feeling?

Investigators will also pose questions of threat, focusing specifically on how the offender acted on the intent to assault—**threat questions**.

- How did the offender threaten the victim?
- Was there a weapon? Describe the weapon.
- Did the offender threaten to use a weapon?
- What exactly was said?
- What commands or orders did the offender give the victim?
- What threats did the offender make to obtain submission?
- Did the offender offer to let the victim live if the victim followed directions?

Next, investigators will begin asking the victim about the **assault** but at this point, it is also important to remind the victim that, although this is the hard part, nothing the victim says will shock the interviewer. Many victims have difficulty talking about the sexual acts, but the information is important and all the details are necessary. This part of the interview will focus on factual questions. For example, the investigator will ask if the offender's penis made contact with the victim, rather than asking if penetration took place. This allows the victim to explain exactly how contact was made, using proper terminology to describe the acts. After the victim describes the sexual acts, investigators will use the victim's language again to describe any acts which may need clarification. This technique is used to ease the victim's embarrassment.

- What did the offender do to the victim?
- What part of the offender touched what part of the victim?
- Did the offender put his penis in or on the victim? Where? Anywhere else?
- Did the offender have an erection?
- Did he have trouble having an erection?
- Did the offender ejaculate? How many times?
- Did he say anything at the time?
- Did the offender tell the victim to put the victim's mouth on the offender's body? Where?
- Did the offender make the victim do other things to the offender's body? Victim's body? What exactly?
- Did the offender have any deformities, scars, tattoos? Where?
- Was the offender circumcised?
- Did the offender use a condom?

- Did the victim see anything on the offender's body that the victim would not have seen if the offender was clothed?
- What did the offender say during the sexual activity?
- Did the offender call the victim by any names?

Lastly, offenders often end a sexual assault by giving orders or warnings to their victims. This is done in hopes of preventing the victim from reporting the crime to authorities. These statements are important to establish the offender's state of mind and, perhaps, identify movement and direction of flight of the offender after the assault. **Termination questions** include the following:

- Did the offender speak after the sexual assault?
- Did the offender brag or make an apology?
- Did the offender tell the victim to follow any instructions (take a shower)?
- Did the offender warn the victim not to move, look, or call anyone?
- What were the offender's actions after the sexual assault?
- Did the offender use the bathroom? Have a snack, take a drink?
- Did the offender turn on the television or radio?
- Did the offender use the telephone?
- How long did the offender remain on the scene after the sexual assault?
- How did the offender leave the scene?
- Did the offender use a car? Leave on foot? Was the offender running or walking?
- Did the offender drive around?
- Did the offender take anything from the scene?
- Did the victim see or hear anything as or after the offender left the scene?

The last part of an interview is important because the victim may look to the investigator for a response and an assessment of guilt. At this time, the investigator must review the victim's statement, making certain the information is accurate and complete. After taking the statement, the investigator may compliment the victim on his or her strength and ability to survive the attack and speak with investigators. They will ask the victim to contact them if any additional details of the assault are recalled in the future and suggest the victim also write down questions to ask the investigator. Lastly, they will thank the victim for assisting and explain the next steps of the investigation.

If the victim has not already been·informed of the availability of rape crisis or other social services, investigators will provide referral information to the victim and offer to make contact on their behalf. The interviewer should also ensure the victim has been given information regarding crime victim rights and the victim is provided a contact telephone number for the investigator. The victim should be reminded to update the investigator if there is a change in addresses or contact numbers for the victim.

4.2.1 Interviewing Children

When interviewing a child, a trained child forensic interviewer should conduct the interview if possible. If a child forensic interviewer is not available, the investigator should take extreme precaution when questioning a child. In addition, welfare services may have qualified individuals who may be able to assist in questioning the child. It is also important to determine the proper setting in which to conduct the questioning. Typically, these types of interviews are conducted in the child's place of residence. This provides a child victim with a secure environment and the investigator is also able to view the child's home and play environment. If the child was victimized in the home or by someone in the home, this would not be an appropriate place to conduct the interview. In these situations, other arrangements should be made to find a suitable location (i.e., a large room with table, chairs, toys, books, paper, crayons, etc.) to conduct the interview.

Similar to other types of interviews, rapport must be established with the child victim. This could be accomplished by spending time playing games, talking, and drawing pictures before starting the interview. After the child appears to be receptive and relaxed in the conversation, the interviewer can begin by explaining interview instructions. These are considered the ground rules, which serve to orient the child to the expectations of a forensic interview and explain permissible responses to the questions posed. Instructions include:

- Give the child permission to say "I do not know."
- Give the child permission to correct the interviewer.
- Give the child permission to say they "do not understand."
- Elicit a promise to always tell the truth.

After the instructions are given to the child, the investigator should focus on making the child comfortable during the interview process.

This could be accomplished by explaining why the interview is being conducted and asking general information about the child. As rapport is built, the crime in question may be tactfully brought into the conversation and/or questioning. Many interviewers use narratives, games, role playing, and/or drawings to assist in acquiring information from a child.

4.3 INVESTIGATION OF SUSPECTS

If the offender was not at the crime scene when the responding officers arrived, the offender may be identified through the victim's description and by developing and prioritizing suspects based on previous arrests, identified profiles, patterns of behavior, composite pictures and photographs or physical evidence. An offender file or **photograph book** of previous offenders may assist in the development of a suspect list. Often, the victim is asked to go to the police station and look through photo books of prior offenders. If possible, the victim is also requested to work with a composite artist to recreate the offender's facial features on a **composite sketch**. Further, the victim will also be asked to develop a offender profile, which may include identifying certain behaviors and traits of the offender. These behaviors and traits include:

- Type of crime (other crimes)
- How the offender approached the victim
- Victim characteristics
- Weapons used in the assault
- "Signature" of the offender
- Verbal information (language used)
- Vehicle, method of entry, exit
- Items taken (souvenir, theft)
- Description of offender
- Type and order of sexual act(s)

Physical evidence must also be examined to assist with the identification of the offender. Physical evidence may include fingerprints, footprints, tool marks, hairs, fibers, and body fluids for DNA analysis, and databank comparison. Latent fingerprints obtained from the crime scene can be matched, using AFIS, to a previously fingerprinted individual. Less commonly, footprints and tool marks may be present at the scene and assist in confirming the identity of a suspect.

It is important to note there may be a delay of several months in receiving the reports of DNA analysis; therefore, it is crucial the victim is aware that this may be a lengthy, but necessary, process.

If the victim is unable to identify the offender in the initial report, a show-up or line-up identification procedure may be necessary. In many cases, victims fear being in the presence of their offender during a line-up, regardless if the offenders can see the victims; therefore, investigators must prepare victims by explaining the procedures and providing reassurance that offenders cannot see them. Victims should be free from pressure or suggestion during the viewing procedure.

If a suspect is identified within a short time after the commission of the crime, the victim will be asked to identify the offender through a show-up procedure. A **show-up** is a one-on-one procedure, which takes place shortly after the assault has taken place. A show-up can be conducted on the street; however, investigators must be cautious regarding how a suspect is portrayed to the victim. If the suspect is in handcuffs or singled-out in any way, it may create selection bias when the victim identifies the offender, creating problems in trial. However, the suspect can be required to speak so the victim can hear the suspect's voice. In addition, if the victim is physically and emotionally stable, he/she may be asked to view the offender for possible identification.

Courts look to both the perceived need of an immediate showing of the defendant and the intent of the police in determining whether a show-up is admissible. A show-up may be suppressed in court if the court determines it was suggestive. Due to the circumstances of a show-up (e.g., length of time, highly distraught victim, and the possibility of identification error), it is more likely a show-up may be more suggestive than a line-up; therefore, it is preferable to conduct a line-up whenever possible. When determining the reliability of offender identification, courts will examine the need to have one-to-one confrontation and the circumstances under which it occurred. Show-ups have been upheld by the courts when the victim had a opportunity to observe the offender during the attack and the victim knew the defendant before the crime.

A **line-up** is conducted if a suspect is identified and a significant amount of time has elapsed after the attack. In a line-up identification process, several suspects are lined in a row and the victim is asked to identify the offender from a set of possible suspects. This process can also be conducted through photograph books or composite drawings. **Photographic line-ups** should not be used if a suspect is in custody, with the exception of extenuating circumstances (i.e., the victim is in intensive care in the hospital). When conducting photo line-ups, it is important to use an array of photos (i.e., black and white, color photos, and even various sizes). While there is no requirement that suspects in a line-up be identical, the techniques of a line-up should not be suggestive. For example, if the suspect is different in size and wears different clothing than other line-up participants, it may be held unnecessarily suggestive and suppressed in court.

Interviews are ultimately conducted to determine the offender's location. To locate the offender, investigators may begin by conducting surveillance of certain locations: home, work, school, relatives, and friends of all suspects. If the victim recognized the offender through prior contact investigators will follow all leads provided by the victim regarding the offender's identity or location whereabouts.

Once a suspect is located, investigators must read the suspect the **Miranda Rights** prior to questioning. Typically investigators will read the statement from a written source and have the suspect waive his or her rights prior to questioning, if desired. An interview will not be conducted if the suspect appears to be under the influence of alcohol or drugs. If suspects utilize their right to remain silent, all questioning must cease. If the suspect later initiates further discussion with police, investigators will again read the Miranda rights and resume with the line questioning. If the suspect asks for an attorney, all questions must cease until an attorney is present. If the suspect has been charged and counsel has been retained or appointed, investigators must wait until the attorney is present before interviewing suspects. All details of the interview must be recorded to demonstrate all aspects of the interview were compliant with the suspects' Miranda Rights. This information will be essential if the suspect's statement is ever challenged in court.

When the investigator begins interviewing the suspect, he/she will explain the nature of the crime, including a description of the time and place of the offense. Often times, the suspect will be asked to tell his or her "side of the story." If the suspect states the victim consented, the suspect will be asked to describe how the victim consented—what exactly indicated the victim's consent to the suspect. If the suspect states the victim consented to the act because of the victim's failure to resist, the suspect will be asked what the victim could have done to stop the assault. If the suspect denies the act, investigators will typically continue the interview to determine whether corroboration can be attained on the suspect's statement. The suspect will also be asked for an alibi, which will be recorded in detail.

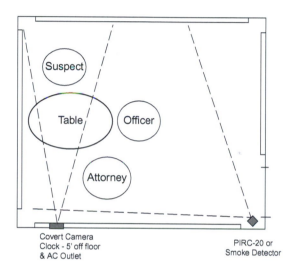

Covert Camera
Clock - 5' off floor
& AC Outlet

PIRC-20 or
Smoke Detector

Figure 4.5 Suggested layout of interrogation room.

The interview of a suspect is a crucial phase of the investigation. The strategy for these interviews will be determined prior to questioning. The interview of the suspect will focus on the consistency of the statements given by the suspect. Investigators will consider the possible motives, profile, and the demeanor of the suspect when adopting a strategy/tactic for the interview. The time, place, and date of the interview are typically recorded. The suspect will be allowed to smoke, drink, eat, rest, and use bathroom facilities as appropriate. The interview room is private and quiet. If there are any windows in the room, they are typically completely covered. The suspect will always be seated closest to the door, which provides a sense of security, feeling as though he or she may easily leave the room any time.

Investigators will begin by building rapport with the suspect. A good objective is for the investigator to find at least three things in common with the suspect, asking general knowledge questions such as: where are you from? Who do you think is going to the Super Bowl this year? They may discuss family, cars, music, etc. If investigators find it difficult to find something in common with the suspect, they will pretend to have something in common (they just need to make sure they are knowledgeable on the subject). By building rapport, the investigators are allowed to assess the suspect's body language such as their posture (legs crossed, arms folded) and changes in body language, specific to the conversation. For example, what was being discussed? Was the suspect's body language more open when discussing certain topics? What topics were discussed when the suspect seemed more guarded and closed off? All of these non-verbal cues assist the investigator in controlling the direction of the interview. Additionally, building rapport provides the investigator with knowledge concerning the things that are most important to the suspect (mother, son or daughter, spouse, money, status). These things may be used by the investigator later to assist in eliciting a confession. The following is a breakdown of the Reid technique's nine steps of interrogation (Reid, 2001; Zulawski and Wicklander, 2001):

Step 1: Direct Confrontation. Lead the suspect to understand that the evidence has led the police to the individual as a suspect. Offer the person an early opportunity to explain why the offense took place.

Step 2: Try to shift the blame away from the suspect to some other person or set of circumstances that prompted the suspect to commit the crime. That is, develop themes containing reasons that will justify or excuse the crime. Themes may be developed or changed to find one to which the accused is most responsive.

Step 3: Try to discourage the suspect from denying his guilt. The more the suspect claims "I didn't do it," the more difficult it is to get a confession.

Step 4: At this point, the accused will often give a reason why he or she did not or could not commit the crime. Try to use this to move toward the confession.

Step 5: Reinforce sincerity to ensure that the suspect is receptive.

Step 6: The suspect will become quieter and listen. Move the theme discussion toward offering alternatives. If the suspect cries at this point, infer guilt.

Step 7: Pose the "alternative question," giving two choices for what happened; one more socially acceptable than the other. The suspect is expected to choose the easier option but whichever alternative the suspect chooses, guilt is admitted. There is always a third option, which is to maintain that they did not commit the crime.

Step 8: Lead the suspect to repeat the admission of guilt in front of witnesses and develop corroborating information to establish the validity of the confession.

Step 9: Document the suspect's admission or confession and have him or her prepare a recorded statement (audio, video or written).

All statements made by suspects are considered either exculpatory or confessional. A **confession** is a statement made by the suspect that admits all the elements of the crime. In this case, the suspect offers no defense and provides information regarding at least one piece of corroborative evidence. An **exculpatory** statement justifies, excuses, or clears the suspect from the alleged crime. When suspects excuse or justify their behaviors, they are likely to make "incriminating statements" which can be useful at trial. For example, if a suspect explains the sexual assault was consensual but a witness heard screams and a struggle, the statement may be considered incriminating.

As an investigator, it is also important to be aware of the offender's motives and rationalizations. Most sex offenders deny allegations or rationalize their behavior to justify their actions. A common rationalization is entitlement. "I paid for the dinner. . ." or "she is my girlfriend, wife, etc." Offender believe they is only taking what is entitled to them. Other offenders may rationalize the victim was "disrespectful." For example, "I gave you drugs. . .you need to repay me with sex." This type of offender believes the victim knew the price for the drugs—not money but sex. Possible recognition of offender typology may assist the investigator by focusing on questions regarding various aspects of the assault. Offenders may be capable of self-delusion and describe romance and enjoyment when the victim reports being terrified. An effective investigative technique is to get into the mind of the offender and feed the rationalizations back to him/her with statements such as:

- "You've got this need which has to be fulfilled and I understand that. . ."
- "You were out of control. . ."

- "Everyone does things they don't mean when they are angry."
- "I'm not saying you're a bad guy"

It is also helpful to provide the offender with possible scenarios leading up to and surrounding the crime. The closer the investigator gets to the real story, the more likely it is the suspect will concede. If the story gets too far from the truth, the suspect will typically speak up, refuting the scenario proposed by the investigator. For example, they may say "No, that's not the way it went" or "No, I did not do anything like that."

Typically, the objective of interviewing a primary suspect is to elicit a confession. Confessions are difficult to refute in court and are rarely dismissed from court proceedings. Although confessions are not needed to prosecute a suspect, under some circumstances there may not be enough physical evidence (DNA, fingerprints, lack of alibi) to link the suspect to the crime; therefore, a confession can be crucial to a case. If the interview is stalled and the suspect continues to deny any part of the crime, certain statements and redirection in questioning may be helpful. The following are a couple of examples that may assist in beginning to elicit an admission of guilt. Investigators may ask, "Did you plan this out or did it just happen on the spur of the moment?" "If a person commits 'said crime,' what type of punishment do you think they should receive?" If suspects respond with anything other than a harsh punishment, this reveals they are quite possibly involved in the crime.

Investigators will often use things that are important to the suspect to initiate guilt. For example, "Don't you think your mother would be really disappointed in you?" Don't you think she would want you to take responsibility for your actions and do the right thing?" At times, investigators will leave the interview room for a while, returning with a stack of documents and files, place them on the table, and continue questioning the suspect. This may imply investigators have incriminating evidence against the suspect and possibly elicit the beginning of a confession. If the interview continues too long and/or the suspect continues to deny the crime without wavering, it may be necessary to discontinue the interview. The suspect will then be released with continued surveillance and brought back in for questioning at a later date. If there is enough evidence to arrest the suspect, the interview may stop and the suspect will be taken into custody.

4.4 USE OF POLYGRAPHS

Sex offenders frequently deny or minimize crimes, as well as past deviant behaviors. According to Trepper and Barrett (1989), there are four types of denials associated with sexual offenders: Denial of facts, denial of awareness, denial of responsibility, and denial of impact. **Polygraphs** can be useful in breaking down the barrier of denial, especially regarding the denial of facts about a sexual crime. Often referred to as a lie detector, a polygraph monitors, measures, and records physiological indicators such as blood pressure, respiration, and heartbeat that may fluctuate abnormally when the suspect is answering questions. Possible questions during a polygraph are centered on culpability and taking responsibility for the behavior.

The second type of denial often claimed by sex offenders includes denial of awareness. Many claim they were unaware of the victim's age or they were under the influence of alcohol and/or drugs at the time of the crime. If deemed important, questions can be formulated to address specific awareness issues. For example, "Did you know the victim was only 13 years old?" or "Do you recall having sexual contact with your daughter?" can be used in an effort to break through very specific denial of awareness issues. Denial of responsibility often involves denial of specific facts and/or denial of awareness. It is not uncommon for an offender to maintain he or she was duped into a sexual encounter with a minor, had been mistakenly identified as the offender, or was under the influence of a substance. Denial of impact is usually related to the minimization of damage (physical and/or psychological) to the victim. Confronting the denial of facts, awareness, and responsibility can easily be addressed with a good polygrapher.

Interviews are typically videotaped, recorded, and witnessed by at least one other law enforcement official (outside of the interrogation room). All suspects' and victims' statements are transcribed or otherwise reduced to writing, and read through by the individual, who corrects any mistakes. The original statement will be properly secured as evidence and a copy will be forwarded to the State's Attorney's office for review (especially concerning suspect's statement).

REFERENCES

Jurkanin, T. J. (1996). Model Guidelines and Sex Crimes Investigation Manual for Illinois Law Enforcement.

Reed, J. (2001). The Reid Technique: Interviews and Interrogations.

Snow, R. L. (2006). *Sex crimes investigation: Catching and prosecuting the perpetrators.* Greenwood Publishing Group.

Sosnowski, D. (2012). Types of Polygraph Used in Sex Offender Testing. Public Agency Training Council.

Trepper, T. S., & Jo Barrett, M. (1989). Systemic treatment of incest: A therapeutic handbook. *No. 15.* Psychology Press.

Zulawski, D. E., & Wicklander, D. E. (2001). *Practical aspects of interview and interrogation.* Ann Arbor: CRC Press.

APSAC Guidelines, (2012). (CASA Interviewing Children retrieved from: <www.azcourts.gov/casa/training> 7/8/13)

CHAPTER 5

Prosecution of Sex Offenders

5.1 CASE STUDIES

5.1.1 Ted Bundy

Theodore Robert "Ted" Bundy faced two murder trials. The first case involved the murders of two Chi Omega sorority sisters, Lisa Levy and Margaret Bowman, near the Florida State University campus in Tallahassee, Florida. The level of publicity surrounding the trial forced prosecutors to relocate the judicial proceedings to Miami, Florida, and the trial date was set for June 25, 1979. The second trial, was for the murder of Kimberly Leach, and was set for January, 1980, in Orlando, Florida.

A plea agreement was negotiated by prosecutors and Ted Bundy's court-appointed defense team prior to the onset of the trials. In exchange for a guilty plea in the murders of Levy, Bowman, and Leach, Bundy would receive a 75 year prison sentence. Bundy, however, refused to publicly admit his guilt, and, at the last moment, turned down the deal. Furthermore, Bundy declined the assistance of his five-member defense team, and chose to represent himself. The trial began, as scheduled, on June 25, 1979.

Bundy was confident in his abilities to defend himself, and felt he would receive a fair trial; however, he was unable to refute two key elements of the case presented against him by the prosecution. First was the eyewitness testimony of Nita Neary, who claimed to have seen Bundy on the night of the murders of Levy and Bowman. While on the stand, she pointed to Bundy as being the man she had encountered fleeing down the stairs of the sorority house. Second was the testimony of forensic odontologist, Dr. Richard Souviron.

Bundy had viciously attacked both women and left bite marks on the buttocks of Lisa Levy. Photographs of the bite wounds were taken at the time of the initial investigation. Dental molds were later made of Bundy's teeth. Dr. Souviron testified the unique indentations left on the victim were a definitive match to the dental physiology of the defendant. Dr. Souviron's testimony offered the best evidence, linking Bundy to the murders.

On July 23, 1979, the jury began deliberations. Less than seven hours later, the jury returned a guilty verdict. The sentencing trial began one week later, on July 30, 1979, Bundy was offered an opportunity to speak on his own behalf to refute the prosecution's death penalty recommendation. During his statement, Bundy claimed he was innocent, and the guilty verdict was the result of media prejudice. He also refused to accept the guilty verdict and told the court it was "absurd to ask for mercy for something [he] did not do." After hearing Bundy's statement, the judge affirmed the prosecution's recommendation and sentenced Bundy to two sentences of death by electrocution in the Florida electric chair.

The second trial against Ted Bundy, for the murder of twelve-year-old Kimberly Leach, began on January 7, 1980, in Orlando, Florida at the Orange County Courthouse. Following the results of the previous trial, Bundy chose not to represent himself and employed the services of defense attorneys Julius Africano and Lynn Thompson. The defense strategy in this second trial was to present a case of not guilty by reason of insanity. The case for an insanity defense was strengthened by Bundy's demeanor throughout the proceedings. He became increasingly agitated, at one point standing yelling at one of the prosecution witness. The prosecution was undaunted and offered 65 witnesses who were able to, in some way, connect Bundy to Leach on the day of her disappearance. As was the case in the first trial, however, it was physical evidence that proved to be the most compelling evidence presented by the prosecution.

Fiber evidence gathered and analyzed during the investigation into the murder of Kimberly Leach definitively connected Bundy to Leach at or around the time of her murder. Fibers taken from Leach's clothing were found in Bundy's white van, as well as on the clothing Bundy was allegedly wearing on the day of her abduction.

On February 7, 1980, after less than seven hours of deliberation, the jury returned with a guilty verdict. The sentencing trial began two days later, on February 9, 1980, the second anniversary of the death of Kimberly Leach. During sentencing phase, Bundy was sentenced to death by electrocution for the third time for the murder of Kimberly Leach.

Bundy immediately launched a series of appeals against his convictions. His execution date was originally set for March 4, 1986, but it was postponed to allow his defense attorney to prepare his appeals. His appeals were repeatedly denied, and the State of Florida issued another death warrant against Bundy. In 1988, following a series of denials by the appellate court system, Bundy began to confess to committing crimes in jurisdictions outside of areas where he had been a prime suspect. He provided only partial information, and investigators were unable to substantiate his claims. In December, 1988, a legal advocate working for Bundy asked families of victims to write to the governor of Florida to request a stay of execution to allow him time to reveal more information. This tactic was not well received, and Florida's then-Governor Robert Martinez refused to allow Bundy to further manipulate the court system and denied a third stay of execution. The last stay was denied by the U.S. Supreme Court on January 17, 1989. Ted Bundy was executed in the electric chair of Raiford Prison on January 24, 1989, at 7:16 a.m.

5.1.2 John Wayne Gacy

The trial of John Wayne Gacy began on February 6, 1980, in the Cook County Criminal Courts Building in Chicago, Illinois. Gacy was indicted for 33 counts of murder. The defense entered a plea of not guilty by reason of insanity. His defense team claimed Gacy was temporarily insane at the time of the murders, but he may have maintained control of his mental faculties before and after the crimes to lure his victims and to dispose of their bodies. More than 100 witnesses were called by the prosecution and the defense, but Gacy did not testify. Among the witnesses were psychiatrists for both the prosecution and the defense who offered testimony regarding Gacy's state of mind. Testimony was also presented by family members of the victims and surviving victims. One witness, Jeffrey Ringall, began vomiting and crying hysterically while describing his rape. He was removed from the courtroom; Gacy showed no emotion.

The trial of John Wayne Gacy lasted five weeks. The jury returned with a guilty verdict after only two hours of deliberation, on March 13, 1980. Gacy was found guilty of 33 counts of murder. He was sentenced to death for 12 murders that were found to have taken place after Illinois passed the post-Furman death penalty statute. In regards to the remaining 21 counts, Gacy was sentenced to serve the remainder of his natural life in prison. Gacy entered two appeals against his convictions, which were denied. Shortly after midnight, on May 10, 1994, John Wayne Gacy was put to death by lethal injection.

5.1.3 Jeffery Dahmer

The murder trial of Jeffrey Dahmer began on January 13, 1992, in Milwaukee, Wisconsin, under strict security, including an eight-foot bulletproof partition that separated him from the courtroom gallery. The case was racially charged because of Dahmer's preference for African-American victims. Tension was heightened by the inclusion of only one African-American juror. Dahmer initially entered a not guilty plea on all counts, despite a 160 confession of his crimes. Against the advice of his attorney, he changed his plea to guilty by virtue of insanity. This drastically altered the defense strategy, forcing his attorneys to detail the gruesomeness of Dahmer's crimes as acts that could only be committed by an insane person. Dahmer's confession was entered into evidence and the prosecution argued that Dahmer was aware of the "evil" nature of his crimes.

The trial lasted two weeks, during which both sides discussed the manner in which Dahmer treated his victims: dismemberment, necrophilia, and cannibalism. On February 17, 1992, the jury took less than five hours to find Dahmer guilty, but sane, of 15 counts of murder. Jeffrey Dahmer was given a maximum sentence under Wisconsin criminal law (Wisconsin abolished the death penalty in the late nineteenth century): 15 consecutive life terms, or 957 years in prison.

Dahmer began serving his sentence in the Columbia Correctional Institution, where he began to study religion and was considered to be a model prisoner. His good behavior allowed him freedoms and privileges within the correctional facility that included integration with other inmates, access to communal areas, and inclusion in regular work details. On November 28, 1994, Dahmer was assigned a work detail with two other inmates: Jesse Anderson, a white supremacist who murdered his wife, and Christopher Scarver, an African-American, schizophrenic murderer. Prison guards left the three alone to perform their duties. The guards returned 20 minutes later to find Scarver had severely beaten Anderson and Dahmer with a broom handle or weight bar. Jeffrey Dahmer's skull had been crushed, and he died in the ambulance while being transported to the hospital. Jesse Anderson died two days later.

5.1.4 Debra Lafave

Debra Lafave entered a plea agreement in the court of Hillsborough County, Florida. She agreed to plead guilty to two counts of lewd and lascivious battery in exchange for avoiding a potential 30 year prison sentence. She received sentence of two years under community supervision and, one year of community supervision with seven years of probation. The sentences would run consecutively, for a total of ten years of probation. After serving two years of community supervision, she had the right to petition the court to have the third year community supervision changed to probation.

The terms of the community supervision were standard conditions for convicted sex offenders in the State of Florida. Lafave was ordered to observe a curfew enforced from 10:00 p.m. until 6:00 a.m. She was also forbidden to come within 1,000 feet of a school, daycare, or any place where children might congregate, and could have no unsupervised contact with any child under the age of 18 without an adult present and court approval. Lafave was also required to enroll in a sex offender treatment program and pay for psychological treatment for her victim. She was forbidden to have any contact with the victim until he was 18 years old. Furthermore, Lafave was ordered to submit a DNA sample to the state sex offender database, and while on probation, to submit to an annual polygraph test.

Lafave was able to get a plea agreement because the victim's mother wished to prevent her son from having to testify. The case drew immediate media attention, credited to the attractive physical appearance of Debra Lafave. As a result of the plea deal granted in Hillsborough County, and also at the request of the victim's mother, similar charges against Lafave were dropped by the prosecutor's office of Marion County, Florida.

In 2009, a Florida trial judge allowed Lafave to have contact with minors after she completed mandatory therapy. In September, 2011, the same judge granted Lafave early release from probation. In August, 2012, this decision was overturned by an appellate court. Lafave entered a request before the Florida Supreme Court, in December 2012, to be removed from probation, and to be allowed her freedom until the court ruled. The court denied the request and reinstated the conditions of her probation. Debra Lafave is currently on probation pending a final ruling by the Florida Supreme Court. If the decision remains in effect, Lafave will be released from parole in 2017.

5.1.5 Trent Mays and Ma'lik Richmond

On March 17, 2013, 17 year-old Trent Mays and 16 year-old Ma'lik Richmond, stars on the Steubenville, Ohio High School football team, were found delinquent on all charges stemming from the rape of an intoxicated female classmate. The presiding judge, a 37 year veteran of the Ohio juvenile court system, came out of retirement to hear the case after the original judge, connected to the football team, recused himself from hearing the case.

The five-day trial included testimony by the victim and witnesses as well as an unprecedented volume of data collected by cybercrime investigators. The victim spent more than two hours on the stand during which time she reiterated her level of intoxication the night of the rape which made her unable to recall details of the alleged attack. The prosecution offered two witnesses who agreed to testify against Mays and Richmond. Both witnesses were granted immunity regarding their level of involvement in exchange for their testimonies. Forensic computer analysts with the Ohio cybercrimes division presented evidence from 13 cellular phones that contained 396,270 text messages, 308,586 photos, 940 video clips, 3,188 phone calls, and 16,422 phone contacts. The Ohio Attorney General stated additional charges of failure to report a felony and tampering with evidence may be filed against other individuals involved in the investigation.

Ma'lik Richmond was sentenced to a minimum of one year in a juvenile detention facility for rape, with a maximum sentence lasting until the offender was 21 years old. Mays was sentenced to a minimum of one year for rape and an additional one year minimum for also being found delinquent on illegal use of a minor in nudity-oriented material. Both deliquents were also forbidden to have contact with the victim until she was at least 21 years old. In subsequent hearings Trent Mays and Ma'lik Richmond were ordered to register as Tier II sex offenders, which according to Ohio State law, requires they register as a sex offender every six months for 20 years; however, unlike adult offenders, the their names will not appear on publicly accessible websites.

5.1.6 Jack Schaap

Jack Schaap faced federal charges relating to his sexual relationship with a 17 year-old parishioner. He waived his right to a grand jury indictment and pled guilty to one count of transporting a minor across state lines for sexual activity. A federal judge went beyond the ten-year sentence recommended by federal prosecutors and, on August 19, 2013, sentenced Schaap to 12 years in a federal prison followed by five years of supervised release.

5.1.7 Aaron Thomas

Aaron Thomas, "The East Coast Rapist," pleaded guilty kidnapping and raping a Leesburg, Virginia woman. He was given two life sentences. Thomas also pled guilty to attacking three teenage girls in Prince William County, Virginia and received an additional three life sentences.

He currently faces an additional 54 counts in Prince George's County, Maryland. The charges include six counts of first-degree rape.

5.1.8 Russell Williams

Former Canadian Forces Colonel Russell Williams pleaded guilty to each of the 88 charges, including the rapes, tortures, and murders of Corporal Marie-France Comeau and Jessica Lloyd. He was stripped of his military rank and released from his military duties. He was given two life sentences without the possibility of parole for 25 years—the maximum penalty allowed under Canadian law.

5.2 LAWS ASSOCIATED WITH SEX CRIMES

1994 – Jacob Wetterling Crimes Against Children and Sexually Violent Offender Registration Act

On the evening of October 22, 1989 in St. Joseph, Minnesota, 11-year-old Jacob Wetterling, his brother Trevor, and his friend Aaron rode their bikes to a neighboring convenience store to purchase a movie and snacks. On their way home, a man wearing a mask and wielding a gun approached the boys. The man told the boys to throw their bikes into a ditch and lie down on the ground. He then asked the boys their ages. After the boys responded, the perpetrator told Trevor to run into the woods and not to look back or he would kill him. Next, the gunman turned to Aaron and told him to run into the woods without looking back or he would kill him as well. Trevor and Aaron ran away, and when they looked back they saw the perpetrator grab Jacob. This was the last time anyone saw Jacob Wetterling alive. To date his where-abouts remain unknown.

(Source: jwrc.org; Retrieved 7/1/13).

Passed as a part of the Omnibus Crime Bill of 1994, the Jacob Wetterling Crimes Against Children and Sexually Violent Offender Registration Act:

• *Established state guidelines to track sex offenders.*
• *Required states to track sex offenders by substantiating their place of residence annually for ten years after their release into the community or every three months for the remainder of their lives if the sex offender was convicted high level sex offense.*

(Source: www.ojp.usdoj.gov/smart/legislation.htm)

1996 – Megan's Law

[On] July 29, 1994, 7 year old Megan Kanka rode her bicycle around her quite neighborhood of West Windsor Township in New Jersey. As she pedaled within close proximity to her suburban home, she noticed her neighbor, Jesse Timmendequas, detailing his boat in his driveway. Megan stopped in the neighbor's driveway and began conversing with Jesse, inquiring about his boat. Unbeknownst to Megan and the rest of the community, Timmendequas was a recently paroled sex offender, who shared his home with two other convicted child molesters. As the two spoke, Timmendequeas asked Megan if she wanted to come inside his house to see his puppy. Once inside, Timmendequas lured Megan into a bedroom, wherein he attempted to touch and kiss the 7-year-old. When Megan tried to run, Timmendequas placed a belt around her neck, strangled, and sexually assaulted her. He later tied plastic bags over her head, placed her body in a toy box, and drove her body to a nearby park. There, he molested her body again and dumped it in a secluded area on the park's grounds. Once Megan's parents realized she was missing later that day, a massive search commenced wherein approximately 500 police officials, 39 firefighters, and a multitude of volunteers combed the area looking for Megan. The next day, Timmendequas confessed to the murder and lead the police to Megan's whereabouts.

(Source: http://www.pennlive.com/news/expresstimes/stories/
molesters5_mainbar.html)

During the mid-1990s every state as well as the District of Columbia, passed Megan's Law. In January of 1996, Congress federally enacted Megan's Law to include:

* *public circulation of information from states' sex offender registries.*
* *information collected under state registration programs to be disclosed for any purpose permitted under a state law.*
* *Required state and regional law enforcement agencies to release the pertinent information necessary to protect the public regarding idividuals registered under a State registration program enacted under the Jacob Wetterling Crimes Against Children and Sexually Violent Offender Registration Act.*

(Source: http://www.ojp.usdoj.gov/smart/legislation.htm)

1996 – The Pam Lychner Sex Offender Tracking and Identification Act of 1996

Pam Lyncher, mother of two, and residential salesperson in Houston Texas received a telephone call one day in 1990 at her place of residence. The caller expressed an interest in looking at a home listed by Pam. The call ended with Pam setting up an appointment to show the house with the male caller. When Pam went to her appointment, her husband accompanied her. When Pam and her husband arrived at the home, Pam stayed in the kitchen and her husband went to another part of the house. At the time of the appointment, a laborer Pam had previously hired entered the house, claiming he had returned to finish the job. When Pam was not paying attention, the laborer grabbed her from behind and attempted to rape her. As a struggle commenced, Pam's husband, Joe, hearing the confrontation, came running to help his wife. As Joe attacked the assailant, Pam escaped, running to a neighbor's house for assistance. The suspect was arrested, convicted, and sentenced to 20 years in prison. The suspect was later found to have been a convicted rapist and child molester who had been released from state prison under a mandatory early release policy.

After Pam's experience, she started working with other victims of sex crimes crime and thereby established an organization called Justice for All (JFA). One of JFA's most profound accomplishments came in 1995 when the Texas Legislature voted to end mandatory early release. Under the new law, criminals convicted after Sept. 1, 1996, became subject to review by the parole board.

(Source: http://realtormag.realtor.org/news-and-commentary/feature/article/ 1997/04/she-refused-give-up)

The Pam Lychner Sex Offender Tracking and Identification Act of 1996 required the Attorney General to establish a national database (the National Sex Offender Registry or 'NSOR') by which the FBI could track certain sex offenders. The law also:

- *Mandated certain sex offenders living in a state without a minimally sufficient sex offender registry program to register with the FBI.*
- *Required the FBI to periodically verify the addresses of the sex offenders to whom the Act pertains.*
- *Allowed for the dissemination of information collected by the FBI necessary to protect the public to federal, state and local officials responsible for law enforcement activities or for running background checks pursuant to the National Child Protection Act*
- *Set forth provisions relating to notification of the FBI and state agencies when a certain sex offender moved to another state.*

(Source: http://www.ojp.usdoj.gov/smart/legislation.htm)

1997 – The Jacob Wetterling Improvements Act

Passed as part of the Appropriations Act of 1998, the Jacob Wetterling Improvements Act made additional strives to amend provisions of the Jacob Wetterling Crimes Against Children and Sexually Violent Offender Registration Act, the Pam Lychner Sex Offender Tracking and Identification Act, and other federal statutes. This law:

- *Changed the way in which state courts make a determination about whether a convicted sex offender should be considered a sexually violent offender to include the opinions not just of sex offender behavior and treatment experts but also of victims' rights' advocates and law enforcement representatives.*
- *Allowed a state to impart the responsibilities of notification, registration, and FBI notification to a state agency beyond each state's law enforcement agency, if the state so chose.*
- *Required registered offenders who change their state of residence to register under the new state's laws.*
- *Required registered offenders to register in the states where they worked or went to school if those states were different from their state of residence.*
- *Directed states to participate in the National Sex Offender Registry.*
- *Required each state to set up procedures for registering out-of-state offenders, federal offenders, offenders sentenced by court martial, and non-resident offenders crossing the border to work or attend school.*
- *Allowed states the discretion to register individuals who committed offenses that did not include Wetterling's definition of registerable offenses.*
- *Required the Bureau of Prisons to notify state agencies of released or paroled federal offenders, and required the Secretary of Defense to track and ensure registration compliance of offenders with certain UCMJ convictions.*

(Source: http://www.ojp.usdoj.gov/smart/legislation.htm)

1998 – Protection of Children from Sexual Predators Act – This Act:

- *Directed the Bureau of Justice Assistance (BJA) to carry out the Sex Offender Management Assistance (SOMA) program to help eligible states comply with registration requirements.*
- *Prohibited federal funding to programs that gave federal prisoners access to the internet without supervision.*

(Source: http://www.ojp.usdoj.gov/smart/legislation.htm)

2000 – The Campus Sex Crimes Prevention Act - Passed as part of the Victims of Trafficking and Violence Protection Act, the Campus Sex Crimes Prevention Act:

- *Required any person who was obligated to register in a state's sex offender registry to notify the institution of higher education at which the sex offender worked or was a student of his or her status as a sex offender; and to notify the same institution if there was any change in his or her enrollment or employment status.*
- *Required that the information collected as a result of this Act be reported promptly to local law enforcement and entered promptly into the appropriate state record systems.*
- *Amended the Higher Education Act of 1965 to require institutions obligated to disclose campus security policy and campus crime statistics to also provide notice of how information concerning registered sex offenders could be obtained.*

(Source: http://www.ojp.usdoj.gov/smart/legislation.htm)

2003 – Prosecutorial Remedies and Other Tools to end the Exploitation of Children Today (PROTECT) Act: Characteristics of this act:

- *Required states to maintain a web site containing registry information, and required the Department of Justice to maintain a web site with links to each state web site.*
- *Authorized appropriations to help defray state costs for compliance with new sex offender registration provisions.*

(Source: http://www.ojp.usdoj.gov/smart/legislation.htm)

2006 - Adam Walsh Child Protection and Safety Act:

- *Created a new baseline standard for jurisdictions to implement regarding sex offender registration and notification.*
- *Expanded the definition of "jurisdiction" to include 212 Federally-recognized Indian Tribes, of whom 197 have elected to stand up their own sex offender registration and notification systems.*
- *Expanded the number of sex offenses that must be captured by registration jurisdictions to include all State, Territory, Tribal, Federal, and UCMJ sex offense convictions, as well as certain foreign convictions.*

- *Created the Office of Sex Offender Sentencing, Monitoring, Apprehending, Registering, and Tracking (SMART Office) within the Department of Justice, Office of Justice Programs, to administer the standards for sex offender notification and registration, administer the grant programs authorized by the Adam Walsh Act, and coordinate related training and technical assistance.*
- *Established a Sex Offender Management Assistance (SOMA) program within the Justice Department.*

(Source: http://www.ojp.usdoj.gov/smart/legislation.htm)

5.3 PROSECUTION OF SEX OFFENDERS

Typically, less than half of sexual assault cases that result in an arrest are prosecuted within the criminal justice system (Spohn and Holleran, 2001). The decision to bring charges against an assailant is based on a combination of victim, suspect, and case characteristics. Prosecutors are more likely to file charges if there is enough physical evidence to connect the suspect to the crime. Additionally, prosecutors often consider the suspect's prior criminal record and the victim's character or behavior at the time of the incident before they proceed with filing charges. This suggests prosecutors are more apt to file charges when they believe the evidence against the suspect is strong, the suspect is liable, and the victim is blameless (Spohn and Holleran, 2001).

Along with the history and character of both the suspect and the victim, some researchers insist the relationship between the suspect and victim plays a role in whether a prosecutor will file charges. Some researchers contend the victim–suspect relationship is an important predictor of case outcomes. Crimes between intimates are perceived as less serious than crimes between strangers (Black, 1976). This opinion, however, is in contradiction to Kingsnorth, MacIntosh, and Wentworth (1999) research, wherein they found that the relationship between the victim and suspect has no effect on the decision to charge.

Beginning in the mid-1970s, many states adopted reforms designed to shift the attention in rape cases from the victim's character to the offender's behavior (Spohn and Horney, 1992). Many reforms included modifications to the definition of rape, such as the removal of the proof of resistance and corroboration that were once required, and the enactment of rape shield laws, in hopes of excluding testimony concerning the victim's sexual history. These reforms were designed to increase the odds of successful prosecution in cases dealing with acquaintance assault and consent discrepancies (Spohn and Horney, 1992). Although research evaluating the impact of the rape law reforms generally concludes statutory changes did not produce the changes that many projected, there is evidence the reforms encouraged arrests and prosecutions in borderline cases concerning acquaintances and consent issues (Spohn and Holleran, 2001).

5.3.1 Plea Bargains

Prosecutors are often referred to as the "gatekeepers of the criminal justice system." They have the freedom to prosecute a case, dismiss a case, or offer a plea bargain. According to the 6th Amendment of the Constitution, however, criminal defendants have the right, to a jury trial. Despite this constitutional right it is estimated that around 90 percent of felony cases are settled through plea bargains.

5.3.2 Use of Victim Testimony

In sex crime cases, the victim's character, behavior, and credibility may play role in charging decisions. These types of cases usually involve little physical evidence connecting the suspect to the crime; and, typically, eyewitnesses are not available to corroborate the victim's testimony. The likelihood of conviction depends primarily on the victim's ability to articulate the nature and context of the assault and to convince a judge or jury that a sexual assault occurred. Thus, prosecutors' assessments of potential conviction and their decisions rest on predictions regarding the way the victim's background history, character, behavior, and articulation of the events may be interpreted and scrutinized by judicial actors and jurors. This leads prosecutors to rely on stereotypes regarding the genuineness of the victim and appropriate behavior associated with being a true victim of a sexual crime. Victims whose backgrounds and behavior conform to these stereotypes are taken more seriously, and their allegations are treated more seriously than victims whose backgrounds and behavior differ from the "stereotypical" sexual assault victim.

5.3.3 Sentencing and Recidivism Rates

Over the past several years in the United States the average sex offender is sentenced to between 6–8 years in prison. Rapists tend to have longer sentences consisting of around 11 years. Those convicted of sexual assault are sentenced to an average of 7 years in prison (Hanson & Bussiere, 1998). Typically, these offenders rarely serve out their entire sentences, usually serving only half of their sentences before being released.

Because sex crimes are under reported, recidivism rates among sex offenders are difficult to determine. Researchers have spent years attempting to determine if sex offenders are more likely to recidivate than other types of criminals such as robbers, drug dealers, white collar criminals, and murderers (Hanson & Bussiere, 1998). Multiple factors typically play a role as to whether or not one continues to sexually offend. These factors are considered dynamic or static. **Dynamic factors** are characteristics or elements in one's life or self that change over time, such as age, marriage, and attitudes. **Static factors** are considered unchangeable characteristics such as biological or genetic traits.

Researchers conclude that, rapists are the most at risk to recidivate (Furby et al. 1989).This may be due to the fact that one of the strongest predictors of sexual recidivism is sexual deviance, which is often associated with individuals who rape. Additionally, criminal lifestyle variables, such as prior sexual offenses and deviant victim choices (children, adolescents, and strangers), may contribute to the propensity to sexually recidivate (Hanson & Bussiere, 1998). Negative emotional states are also found to be contributors to the onset of a sexual offense and/or cycle.

Offenders who accept responsibility for their actions, express remorse, and conform to treatment are typically at a lower risk of recidivism than those who deny any wrongdoing. This motivation to change is difficult to assess, however, since many offenders may benefit from the appearance of remorse, and most have the social capability to gain the trust of a sympathetic clinician (Hanson & Bussiere, 1998).

5.4 SEX REGISTRIES AND DETERRENCE

In the United States, sex offender registries are conducted at the local or state level. Typically, sex offenders are required to register with local law enforcement of any state, municipality, territory, or tribe in which they reside, retain employment, or attend school. Every locality makes its own determination as to who is required to register, what information those individuals are required to provide, and which offenders will be posted on the jurisdiction's public registry online site (Sex Offender Registration Notification in the United States: Current Laws and Issues, U.S. Department of Justice 2012). Most jurisdictions limit their registration and notification requirements to those convicted of sex offenses and non-parental kidnapping of a minor. Some states include other dangerous or violent offenders on their registration and notification systems (Sex Offender Registration Notification in the United States: Current Laws and Issues, U.S. Department of Justice 2012).

Although the implementation of residency restrictions and notifications varies across states and jurisdictions, lawmakers identify areas that are off-limits to sex offenders (Nobles, Levenson, and Youstin, 2012). These areas may be referred to as hot spots and buffer zones (Barnes, 2011; Nobles, Levenson, and Youstin, 2012). **Hot spots** are specific locations from which sex offenders are restricted, such as parks, playgrounds, childcare facilities, schools, bus stops, and the current location of the offender's victim (Barnes, 2011 Nobles; Levenson, and Youstin, 2012). A **buffer zone** is considered an area where sex offenders are prohibited from residing. Buffer zones typically range from 500 to 5,000 feet of the perimeter of the state's specified hot spots (Barnes, 2011; Nobles, Levenson, and Youstin, 2012). Specific laws related to residency restrictions may vary across jurisdictions; however, the overall goal of preventing sex crimes remains constant (Sample and Bray, 2003).

Various researchers and lawmakers rationalize residency restrictions distance offenders from potential victims by limiting access to specific locations (Berenson and Applebaum, 2011). The assumption is the proximity to potential victims leads to an increase in recidivism among sex offenders (Tewksbury and Mustaine, 2006). This view may be attributed to the criminological principle of **distance decay**, which proposes offenders generally commit crimes with less frequency the greater the distance from their residence (Berenson and Applebaum, 2011). This concept retains merit; however, no empirical data exists that supports the assumption that a particular location of an offender's residence increases recidivism (Duwe, Donnay, and Tewksbury, 2008).

5.4.1 Research and Unintended Consequences of these Laws
The implementation of residency restrictions is to provide protection and safety to the community; however, numerous unintended consequences

have arisen as a result of these laws. These ramifications not only affect the offender but also the community. Consequences include difficulty securing housing, clustering of sex offenders, limited resources, and emotional and financial distress (Levenson and Cotter, 2005).

Sex offenders face obstacles such as finding a place to reside because housing options (low-income housing or residing with family/ friends) may be located in restricted zones. This may result in the clustering of sex offenders in limited unrestricted zones. In Iowa, one hotel claimed to house 23 sex offenders because it was one of the very few places sex offenders could legally reside (Levenson and Cotter, 2005).

Furthermore, as a result of limited housing options, offenders are often forced to reside in rural areas (Duwe, Donnay, and Tewksbury, 2008; Levenson and Hern, 2007; Walker, 2007). This typically places offenders far from social, community, and governmental resources (Duwe, Donnay, and Tewksbury, 2008; Levenson and Hern, 2007; Walker, 2007). Social services and other community assistance organizations are typically concentrated in urban locations (Duwe, Donnay, and Tewksbury, 2008; Levenson and Hern, 2007; Walker, 2007). This may pose difficulties for offenders when attempting to reach mental health and substance abuse services, or probation and parole offices. Restriction to rural areas may also impede the offender's ability to find adequate employment and retain supportive social networks (Berenson and Applebaum, 2011; Walker, 2007).

Sex offenders who are subject to residency restrictions often experience emotional instability as a result of limited housing options and inadequate resources. Researchers indicate mood disorders are prevalent among these types of offenders (Jeglic, Mercado, and Levenson, 2012). A study conducted by Jeglic, Mercado, and Levenson (2012) revealed that, given the financial, legal, and psychological consequences of a sex offence conviction, sex offenders experience moderate levels of hopelessness and depression (Jeglic, Mercado, and Levenson, 2012). Studies suggest those with lower levels of hope are at a higher risk of recidivism (Martin and Stermac, 1999). These psychological consequences, which may contribute to increased recidivism, are counterintuitive to the purposes of reducing sex crimes (Nobles, Levenson and Youstin, 2012).

In addition, these laws have the potential to place a tax burden on the community-registering and tracking sex offenders (Durling, 2006). The boundary restrictions, which so often extend into neighboring counties and states, cause cross-jurisdictional policy issues that are not easily resolved (Chajewski and Mercado, 2009). An additional problem is the decline in property values in the community that a sex offender resides. Housing prices within the vicinity of a sex offender's home typically decline by over 5,000 dollars (Walker, 2007). Thus, the unintended consequences of sex offender laws goes beyond impacting just the individuals. It can have a negative effect on the community, as well (Chajewski and Mercado, 2009; Duwe, Donnay and Tewksbury, 2008; Freeman, 2010; Levenson and Hern, 2007).

5.5 REHABILITATION

Rehabilitation of sex offenders over the last several years has been centered on **cognitive behavioral therapy**.

Cognitive therapy proposes maladaptive behaviors and disturbed mood states and/or emotions are the result of irrational thinking patterns. These thinking patterns are referred to as **automatic thoughts**. Instead of reacting to the reality of a situation, an individual reacts to his or her own distorted observation of the situation. For example, a person may conclude he or she is "worthless" simply because of failing to get a date. Cognitive therapists attempt to make their patients aware of these distorted thinking patterns, or cognitive distortions, and attempt to alter these perceptions—a process termed cognitive restructuring. **Behavioral therapy**, or behavior modification, trains individuals to replace undesirable behaviors with healthier behavioral patterns. Cognitive-behavioral therapy incorporates the cognitive restructuring associated with cognitive therapy and behavioral modification techniques of behavioral therapy. Cognitive behavioral therapists, therefore, work with the patient to identify both the thoughts and behaviors that are causing distress, and help individuals readjust their behavior.

In conjunction with various forms of therapy, polygraph testing is often administered to sex offenders who have been released from jail or prison. This type of testing is typically broken down into three sections: sexual history disclosure, maintenance, and monitoring.

The **Sexual History Disclosure** examination is utilized to explore and extract previous involvement in sexual behavior. The sexual history information can be helpful in facilitating treatment and assessing risk factors. In addition to sexual history disclosure, polygraph examinations may be used for compliance issues concerning probation and treatment (**Maintenance Testing**) and specific issues dealing with new sex offences (**Monitoring Testing**).

A Maintenance Examination is utilized to monitor sex offender's activities, behavior, and truthfulness while on probation or parole. It is generally administered every three to six months to ensure offender compliance with conditions set forth by probation and parole. Compliance with treatment conditions, such as requiring an offender to not associate with children, view pornography, use alcohol or illegal drugs, and to abstain from specific sexual behaviors, can be effectively monitored.

A multidisciplinary approach is essential for polygraph testing to be the most effective. The common goal for the use of polygraphs in the rehabilitation of sex offenders is the prevention of new victims. This objective is acquired through constant and open communication between probation/parole agents, law enforcement agencies, therapists, and polygraph examiners to ensure its success in the prevention of future offending.

5.6 CONCLUSION

Despite the fact that sex offenders are considered the least unlikely criminals to recidivate, this does not make these criminals any less frightening. Many individuals across the world are affected directly or indirectly by a sex offender. This book is intended to provide the reader with, not only the proper knowledge and steps required in the investigation of sex offenders and sex crimes, but also knowledge and awareness in the hopes of detecting and/or preventing sexual offenders and sex crimes.

REFERENCES

Barnes, J. C. (2011). Place a moratorium on the passage of sex offender residence restriction laws. *Criminology & Public Policy, 10*(2), 401–409.

Berenson, J. A., & Applebaum, P. S. (2011). A geospatial analysis of the impact of sex offender residency restrictions in two New York counties. *Law & Human Behavior, 35*, 235–246.

Brantingham, P., & Brantingham, P. (1995). Criminality of place. *European Journal on Criminal Policy and Research, 3*(3), 5–26.

Black, D. (1976). *The behavior of Law*. New York: Academic Press.

Cassia, S., & Holleran, D. (2004). Prosecuting Sexual Assault: A Comparison of Charging Decisions in Sexual Assault Cases Involving Strangers, Acquaintances, and Intimate Partners.

Chajewski, M., & Mercado, C. C. (2009). An evaluation of residence restriction functioning in town, county, and city-wide jurisdictions. *Criminal Justice Policy Review, 20*(1), 44–61.

Durling, C. (2006). Never going home: Does it make us safer? Does it make sense? Sex offenders, residency restrictions and reforming risk management law. *The Journal of Criminal Law & Criminology, 97*, 317–380.

Duwe, G., Donnay, W., & Tewksbury, R. (2008). Does residential proximity matter? A geographic analysis of sex offense recidivism. *Criminal Justice and Behavior, 35*, 484–504.

Freeman, N. J., Sandler, J. C., & Socia, K. M. (2009). *A Time Series Analysis on the Impact of Sex Offender Registration and Community Notification Laws on Plea Bargaining Rates, 22*, 153–165.

Freeman, N. J., & Sandler, J. C. (2010). The Adam Walsh Act: A false sense of security or an effective public policy initiative. *Criminal Justice Policy Review, 21*(1), 31–49.

Hanson, K. R., & Bussiere, M. T. (1998). Predicting relapse: A meta analysis of sexual offender recidivism studies. *Journal of Consulting and Clinical Psychology, 66*, 348–362.

Jeglic, E., Mercado, C., & Levenson, J. (2012). The prevalence and correlates of depression and hopelessness among sex offenders subject to community notification and residence restriction legislation. *American Journal of Criminal Justice, 37*(1), 46–59.

Kingsnorth, M., & Wentworth (1999). Sexual Assault: The role of prior relationship and victim characteristic in case processing. *Justice Quarterly, 16*, 275–302.

Levenson, J., & Cotter, L. (2005). The impact of sex offender residence restrictions: 1,000 feet from danger or one step from absurd. *International Journal of Offender Therapy and Comparative Criminology, 49*, 168–178.

Levenson, J., & Hern, A. L. (2007). Sex offender residence restrictions: Unintended consequences and community reentry. *Justice Research & Policy, 9*, 59–73.

Martin, K., & Stermac, L. (1999). Measuring hope: Is hope related to criminal behavior in offenders. *International Journal of Offender Therapy and Comparative Criminology, 54*(5), 693–705.

Nobles, M. R., Levenson, J. S., & Youstin, T. J. (2012). Effectiveness of residence restrictions in preventing sex offender recidivism. *Crime & Delinquency, 58*(4), 491–513.

Sample, L. L., & Bray, T. M. (2003). Are sex offenders dangerous? *Criminology and Public Policy, 3*(1), 59–82.

Spohn, C., & Holleran, D. (2001). Prosecuting Sexual Assault: A comparison of charging decisions in sexual assault cases involving stranger acquaintances and intimate partners. *Justice Quarterly, 18*(3), 651–688.

Sphon, C., & Horney, J. (1992). *Rape Law Reform: A grass roots revolution and its impact*. New York: Plenum.

Sex Offender Registration Notification the United States: Current Laws and Issues, U.S. Department of Justice, 2012.

Tewksbury, R., & Mustaine, E. E. (2007). Collateral consequences and community re-entry for registered sex offenders with child victims: Are the challenges even greater? *Journal of Offender Rehabilitation, 46*, 113–131.

Walker, J. T. (2007). Eliminate residence restrictions for sex offenders. *Criminology & Public Policy, 6*(4), 863–870.